I GREW UP
IN
WOLVERTON TOO

Compiled and edited by
Ruth Edwards and Bryan Dunleavy

a second collection of thoughts and reminiscences from
thos who spent their growing years in Wolverton

I GREW UP IN WOLVERTON TOO

Published by Magic Flute Publications 2012

ISBN 978-1-909054-10-3

Magic Flute Publications
Magic Flute Artworks Limited
231 Swanwick Lane
Southampton SO31 7GT

www.magicflutepublications.co.uk

Contents

cover photograph - an old steam train coming round the bend at Wolverton Station © Paul Gray
back cover photograph - Edwardian Church Street blends into 21st century Church Street © Will Hawkins

List of Illustrations

Ring out the Bells

A comment, a quip,
A friendly jibe
Ring out the bells
Our friend has died

No more the banter
No more the craic
Ring out the bells
We want him back

The laughter, the stories
The photo's we loved
Ring out the bells
And send up the doves

A book full of memories
For generations to share
Ring out the bells
To show that we care

Communities united
Friends in grief
Ring out the bells
It's beyond our belief

We'll remember the laughter
We'll remember our Ron
Silence the bells
For Our friend has gone

Sheila Higginbotham

We would like to dedicate this book to the memory of Ron Baker, well-known in the Bradwell, Wolverton and Stony Stratford area, who died quite suddenly and unexpectedly at the end of 2012. His warmth and wit, which lit up all our lives, will be sadly missed.

Acknowledgements

Photographs and illustrations have been contributed by the following:
Harvey Allen: The Old Cricket Pavilion p63, The Wolverton Express p129, Wolverton Express Staff p130. Ron Baker: Football spectators from the 1950s p66, Steve Baker: Roller Skating in the Agora p41. Pete Beale: Canal Development p172. Julia Bennett: Science & Art Institute in its prime p59. Nick Carter: Mr King and Alf Nash at the Bakery p38, Sellicks Garage on the Stratford Road p122. Stephen Clarridge: © Wolverton Park Development p166, Wolverton Park Today p173. Bryan Dunleavy: © First Day at Wolverton Station - September 1838 p.3, Lunchtime at works p19, Going home p20, Outside Muscutt & Tompkins p22, Buckingham Street -Radcliffe Street Corner p29, Eady's Butcher Shop p32, Kings Bakery c. 1960 p33, Rubbish Collection Day p159, Down Radcliffe Street 40 years ago p49, Football at Wolverton Park p65, Newt Pond at the old allotments p80. Chris Gleadell: © New Statues p 141, p143. Paul Gray: © Cover photograph. John Hawkins: Wolverton Station Entrance p154. Will Hawkins Agora from Square p43, Church street, back cover. Susan Hay: BR Carnival Float p85. Barrie Holland: M1 Service Area Today p112. John Holland: Church St and the newly constructed Agora p39. Linda Kincaid : A View of the Little Streets in 1950 p 4. Terry Levitt: Wolverton's Fire Crew p56, Stairs Leading to the Platform p150, Station Entrance with Taxis p151,Train of Events Film Location 2 March 1949 p153. Geoff Lloyd: Market Hall Gates p6, Market hall interior 1980 p16. Philip Marsh © The New Station at Wolverton p158, Jackie Nott: © Agora under construction p28, Gas showroom, Buckingham Street p30, View to North of Square p31, View after clearance p31, Kings under demolition 1975 p35, Science and Art Institute after fire p57, McCorquodale's Printing Works p67,Moon Street School Pool p116. Helen Orme: © BR Main Gate p62, The Market Hall on Creed Street p18. Kim Pavey: Old railway carriage on allotment p81. Elaine Pilcher: Science and Art Institute on Fire p53. Lee Proudfoot McCorquodale Centenary Brochure p69. John Reed: Royal Train Shed p147. John Stephenson The "Pineapple" under construction p64. Karen Waugh: George Pedley Hairdresser p125. Phillip Webb: Electrolux Fire p50, Works Offices Fire p52, LNWR Exhibition Stand made in Wolverton p86. Julie Woodruff: A Model of Wolverton's Third Station p155.

Part One:

Room for Change

Part One
ROOM FOR CHANGE

First Day at Wolverton Station - September 1838

175 years ago Wolverton, a quiet, underpopulated rural community in North Buckinghamshire, began its life as a railway town. The railway line is still in use and some trace of railway maintenance workshops retain the railway connection, but in the past 30 years Wolverton has moved on. Some would say it has moved with the times; others regret the passing of a once dominant industry in this community.

Many of these thoughts are reflected in this second collection of conversations about Wolverton. For the most part this book focuses on the period from the 1970s onward when the railways were in decline and the new city of Milton Keynes was growing in size and importance. Wolverton changed in the post-war years from being the largest and dominant town in North Bucks to a northern outpost of Milton Keynes.

As with the first book, the conversations range from the trivial to the profound, from complaint to celebration, from nostalgia to realism but overall, as is our intention, they leave on record a unique social history of the town that is Wolverton.

Older Wolverton

The Little Streets

The first significant change to the town came in the mid 1960s when the original railway cottages were cleared by the Council. There was a prevailing urge across the country in the 1960s to sweep away Victorian buildings and replace them with something modern, such as a high rise building of concrete, steel and glass. Wolverton was not immune.

This view from some works offices offers a good view of those early terraces Creed Street, Ledsam Street and Glyn Square.

A View of the Little Streets in 1950

Linda K. I bought this picture yesterday at Gdad. Apparently it is the Little Streets taken from the Works. I love the photo but am confused by where exactly it may have been taken from .Would the street facing the advertisements be Stratford Road?

Ian H. Spot on Linda , even got a corner of the market!!! Great photo!!

Chris G. Could have been taken from upstairs in the Works Canteen.

Ian H. Maybe a chimney sweep

Jane B. Oh wow - great pic Linda. Take it Chris that the road bottom left is what we know as Creed Street?

Bryan D. That was a good find Linda. Probably taken in the 1950s or earlier. The Players Ad will date it. And yes Jane that is the original Creed St.

John H. good pic

Ruth E. Great pic x

Sandra & Steve A. Fantastic picture

Brian E. Amazing picture

Jill G. fab pic, love the ads on the end of the houses.

Sue L. Brilliant picture xx

Bryan D. I think I can date this at around 1950. Certainly not much later and perhaps earlier. These billboard ads were all around at this time - Guinness for Strength, the Persil ad which showed one boy with a slightly grey "white" shirt, and the Player's Please which still featured the naval rating. Players were probably the most popular cigarette brand back then. The Creed Street cottages in the front were built in 1840 and Ledsam Street and Glyn Square in the same period. The Ledsam Street terrace you can see in the middle were quite cramped and after a decade or two they knocked together two cottages on the near side into one. In the bottom right hand corner is the wall around the old school playground. The shed roof was cover for some market stalls. The Training School had not been built at this date so the buildings facing Glyn Square are the Works Laundry. Once again thank you Linda for this photo.

David Wm. good photo

Linda K. Thank you so much for all the info. I remember the market well but never saw the Little Streets so found it hard to place the picture . I never imagined that there would have been advertisements on the side of the terraces. Stratford Road was a lot more interesting back then!

Bryan D. I think there were advertising hoardings on the other side too.

Jackie N. This is the best picture I've seen of the "little Streets" what a great find, thanks for sharing!

Edith H. So which one was Young Street Bryan?

Pam B. Young St was the first street up from the railway yards,the one with the drying green where the washing was hung out to dry.

Bryan D. Young street is not visible in this photo - being off to the right as Pam B. described.

Edith H. Thank you both. My memory is not very good at the moment.

Pamela J. Oh god I remember the little streets my Mum lived in Ledsam St. with my brother and my step father. Love the photo.

Steve A. Fantastic picture! Thanks for posting it. I'm guessing it was taken from the works canteen.

The Market Hall

The Market Hall on Creed Street was a central feature of Wolverton life every Friday. The market was held here from 1906 until the Agora opened in 1980. This photograph was probably taken after the last day.

Market Hall Gates

Geoff Ll. How about this as as Idea for replacing the Agora? Happy memories walking round on a Friday with Mum.
Lesley W. That was what we called a market !!!! Happy memories.. thanks.
Jane B. Oh wow - just as I remembered it - happy days - thanks Geoff !!!

Mark B. I remember the distinctive smells of the place and going around with my mum and gran, big sis and twin brother. As Jane says happy days.

Ruth E. Happy days Horace Barber (Barleys Fruit Stall) trundling in with Peter & the truck ......

Ant K. Lovely photo

Ruth E. Ant did you know there is a picture of Kings Bakery in IGUIW book?

Sheila St. Cheap Jacks stall?

June L. The Best!

John H. The sign says, This Market closes to-day, Reopens next week AGORA.

Pamela J. Wolverton Market . Fri was a good lunch time spending wages on new shoes loved it the market that is John it should say agora closed market opens next week (whoops)

June L. Me & my mum use to go every Friday to the Material Stall as we were both machinists although mum still made most of my clothes. We'd buy most of our weeks shopping there, our meat from Greens butcher, our vegetables, toys for Terry, our comfy slippers, well mum did, I don't think I wore them when I was young, I use to get told off if I waked on Lino with Stilettos, no fitted carpets in those days. No decimal money, all pounds shilling & pence, every thing was marked ending with 99 eg £1.99 £4.99 mind you that was for something expensive most things would be coppers in the market then, lbs & ounces, so much easier, it seemed like directly after the Changeover prices shot up & never stopped.

Anthony Z. Superb photo, now this does bring back some great memories

Margaret C. Stratford road entrance has brought back many memories and that's where the fish man was with his weekly treat of winkles.

Mervyn J. Gas lamps with brass shades. The lamps hissed.

Donna S. Fantastic photo... and what memories.. loved going there .. walking around looking at all that was offered. sometimes would save pocket money from week before so could go get myself something ...

Margaret C. Had op on Thursday laying here feeling sorry for myself so thanks for the add of this photo gave me something else to think about .

Brian E. Where you could get the best fishcakes ever.

Pamela J. I loved walking on the floor boards they made such a smashing sound cannt even get close to it today

June L. Wish you well soon Margaret x. Yes these photos prove they were better times for us, kids eat their veg without trouble then, except for cabbage but that was the schools fault. It was boiled to death & stunk the schools out.

Donna S. lol June.. for me it as brussel sprouts .. oh god can't stand them. or squash,.turnip,swede, anything else I'm game for....

June L. We were certainly happier shopping, didn't get stressed out like they do these days. Everything was @ hand & didn't get moved around so you couldn't find what you were looking for, shopping worked out much cheaper too, because we were sensible not to spend over our limits.

Donna S. You could enter either Stratford road side or Creed Street... seem to recall either being with my gran or by myself.. mum worked at Engineers so I would stop there first see if she wanted me to get anything..

Margaret C. Thank you June. Was very impressed with the breast care team and theatre staff at the MK treatment centre they were very kind and caring. X The first stall in from Creed Street was a shoe stall.

June L. They are Margaret, two of my friends have just gone through having their breasts removed, such a lot of it about, I'm lucky touch wood as my biopsy wasn't cancer thank God.

Donna S. Speaking of shoes... love the smell of a shoe store .. there was a small one in town where i used to live recently, went in there and was taken back 30 years... the smell, clark shoes....the strap leather shoe we wore for school.. loved those... thats back in day where like most things were made to last... you outgrew before you outwore...

Pam F. I had one removed in 2008 and i'm still going strong x

June L. Donna I know what you are saying, I don't like turnips & I didn't like parsnips until I tried roasting them, I think it's how veg is cooked, I love Brussels & runner beans Only when they are cooked to perfection & most Resturants & Chefs don't know how to cook them, it's all about presentation with most Chefs.

Pam F. Totally agree June

Donna S. I'm sure your probably right as i used to hate liver .. but love it now .. but nope aint gonna get me to eat brussel sprouts.. or turnip.. nope not happening...

Donna S. Speedy recovery Margaret, think only positive thoughts....

Pam F. Positive is the only way. It worked for me, with the support too of my family and friends of course. Margaret if you're welcome to chat with me PM me if you want to. x

June L. That's nice

Margaret C. I am very lucky as far as I know it's just a tissue infection which they have removed. Will know for sure at next app . Thank you x

Ian H. That is one super photo, keep them coming!!

Ruth E. Get well soon Margaret xx

Ian H. Keep it up Margaret XXX

Elizabeth M. Oh what a lovely memory. Meeting my mum off the Bradwell bus along the front at Wolverton, with two kids in the pram. Then doing our weekly visit to the market for veg, meat and anything else that took our fancy. Bottom of the pram loaded we would then walk back up to Gloucester Road for a cup of tea. Bit of a ritual but priceless memories.

Margaret Ck. Loved the old market..the tea room up in the right corner....

Vivienne B. Lovely nostalgic picture, happy memories, always ran past the fish counter, can't stand the smell of fish, Mum always brought our meat from the butcher in there, makes we wonder what it would look like if it was still there today.

Margaret Ck. Remember Tony Sweet, the fabric guy, used to make a lot of my girls clothes ...loved to sew.

Ian H. ....and his "lad" Billy Sharman Margaret !!!!

Margaret Ck. The name ring a bell Ian, was he a Wolverton kid or from Northampton with Tony, I used to see Christine Weir? in there too, she liked to sew.

Lesley W. Was that Bill Sharman from the top of Windsor Stret Ian? I went to school with Michael and there was also a Bernard I recall.

Sheila S. And a Patsy Lesley.

Lesley W. Yes and now I remember a Jennifer as well.

Ian H. He lived in the Little Streets before moving to Windsor St Margaret . He was Tony's lad for quite a long time................or was it Bill Green from Church Street? Perhaps one took over from the other??

Bryan D. Billy Sharman was in our class sometimes with Miss Faux in our first year at Junior School. For some reason or other she really took against him and he only had to move in his seat before she was on to him. The poor kid seemed to get in trouble all the time without trying.

Ian H. Thinking more about Billy Sharman, perhaps he worked for the sweet stall before he helped out with the material seller. In any event both Billy's worked on the market in the 50's

Ian H. It almost looks like a drawing...................and not a Billy in sight:-)

Pam F. I remember Billy, he had a bit of a reputation from what i remember. Wasn't there a Margaret Sharman as well,

Lesley W. I don't recall a Margaret.

Vivienne B. I went to school with Pamela Sharman from Windsor St.

Pam F. Don't remember a Pamela Sharman.

Lesley W. Nor me ..Jennifer Michael Bernard and Patsy.

Vivienne B. May not be same family Pam, She is the same age as me 57yrs, I think she had an older brother.

Sarah T. That was just by my back gate l loved the market I can smell it now !

Becca H. I remember Pam Sharman well. She lived in Windsor Street and went out with Clive Connor (Conk) for quite a while. x

Vivienne B. Thanks Becca thought I had lost the plot lol x

Sandra & Steve A. OMG memories flooding back fantastic xx

Margaret C. Excuse my language but Billy was a bugger. Also thought he was a good catch was older than me but recall some antics down the park. He lived up near my Uncle Charlie in Windsor Street.

Donna S. Always hoped someone had a picture of the market... lots of good memories I believe for all of us of a certain time..

Stephen Ce. Anything better than Agora used to like Wolverton market

Elizabeth M. The market had character not like the Agora.

Susan B. I enjoyed walking around the Friday market with my mum as a child, going to our normal veg store and fishmonger outside for our Friday dinner which was cod most weeks with potatoes and peas with lots of parsley sauce, occasionally chips, once the market had move to the agora it wasn't the same feeling anymore. Wouldn't it be nice if we could turn back time and have Wolverton back as we all liked it

Del R. Just inside on the right, cockles, yum!

Ian H. It was on the left in my days Del, white aproned tall man with collar and tie...............and a moustache like me;-)

Ron B. Yea dodgy looking bloke. I remember him now.lol

Ian H. Oy Ronnie boy, now you are telling porkies (from Green's no doubt ;-))

Susan B. Very often stopped and got cockles for my dad as it was his Friday treat

Pat B. That's a great photo of the old market. I can remember the cockle stall on the left and the old gas lamps inside, My friend and I used to meet every Friday come rain or shine with our Silver Cross prams to search Tony Sweet's remnants to make our own clothes and buy our veg. from Botterill's stall.... We still meet to this very day for a look round the market and a coffee. But without the prams.

Ruth E. I worked on Barleys stall in the market and used to watch Botterill's put green tomatoes in bags on the back and then fill them with red ones from the front, chat the ladies up & guess what? They never noticed lol....

Pat B. I must have been one of those Ruth. But Mr Barley too gave a bit of flannel. That's market traders for you.

Ruth E. Oh Mr B for sure could flannel his ladies x

Debbie W. My god i remember trawling around that place!

Ron B. Must be a common thing with guys called Mr B Ruthie.xx

Margaret Ck. June I'm roasting parsnips right now...love them... and I didn't used to like them...have potatoes, carrots, onion and parsnips all nicely browning around my roast..lol

Brian E. And, on Fridays, it was always packed, wasn't it. No matter what the weather.

Ruth E. Think maybe it is x

Brian E. You can roast carrots as well. keep an eye on them tho.

Becca H. Roasted whole red onions with roasted carrots are yum!

with a few spots of honey and a very light random sprinkle of rock salt about half way through cooking x

June L. I'll try that Becca.

Keith T. In those days gates shut meant we are closed not please climb over and help yourself.

Gary C. I used to go with my nan every Friday and I would hold her hand all the way down from Gloucester Road, she would buy me a Dinky toy car and a bunch of grapes, once I had those I wouldn't hold her hand any more (so she old me).

June L. Naughty Gary, poor Nan.

Jackie N. what a great picture! Used to go to the fish stall for smoked haddock for Friday tea -and always at the fabric stall , as Mum and I made our clothes(I started sewing when I was about 12)

Barbara L. Pig trotters were sold too we think?

Pam F. Yes Mum used to buy them and cook them for my Dad. Oh and tripe horrid stuff. And lights for the cats. might have spelt that wrong x x

Lynn A. My Grandad always used to bring me a bag of white chocolate rainbow buttons from the sweet stall, cos Mum said I didn't need them.

Brian E. Oh I remember those rainbow bottons, & when they were gone you still had the coloured bits in the bottom of the bag.

Diane K. Now there's a memory me and my sis used to love going to the market and look at the toy stall.

Bryan D. Anyone remember what colour was used to paint these gates? Was it BR maroon, or were they painted black with creosote? Or were they unpainted and just a silvery grey?

Terry L. I thought they were Green, but don't know why I think that

Bryan D. You may be right. Maroon would show up darker in the photo.

Harvey A. Without being certain I would have thought maroon, Brian. For a period in the 1950s there was a cheapjack merchant on the stall behind, using his gift of the gab to off-load his merchandise onto the unsuspecting public, as I know to my then teenage cost!

Phillip W. Is maroon the same colour as what was on the works gates?

Pamela L. Hi Bryan pretty sure they were maroon.

Hazel C. Was only talking about this gate the other day and the fish monger's stall on the right as you enter the gates....

Bryan D. Thanks all. That confirms my own thoughts.I;m doing a drawing based on this so a dirty maroon will be about right.

Elaine H. With you Terry. Green came straight into my mind.

Del R. Get us some cockles.

Lynne P. Wow the ol' market ...good days ...now there's. nothing thats gonna be remembered, like the market ..

Janet B. My first thought was Green as Terry and Elaine have said.

Ken C. Andrew - can you please type in the words on the sign - I cannot make them out. The fishmonger was my uncle - the family used to live at 14, Windsor street in the early 1900's until mid-50's. In the 50's ands 60's he lived in Northampton.

Janet B. Ken it looks like it says.This Market Close's Today. Re-opens next week at the Agora.

Bryan D. I don't know whose photo this is but it looks like the last day of the market hall. If anyone knows the week it closed for the last time this would date it accurately.

Jackie N. I'm thinking green gates too-maroon doesn't sound right ..…

Elaine H. They def were not maroon!

Ian B. Always possible that over time they were painted different colours, but I remember them being green.

Elaine H. Green it is then.

Bryan D. OK I'll go for green, but I would imagine a rather dull, dark green.

Barbara L. Maroon

Bryan D. Confused dot com!

Harvey A. Perhaps we are all right. Different colour at different times?

Pamela L. Hi all. I think Harvey is right the younger folks seem to think green us oldies maroon. That should confuse you even more

Terry L. Ha ha Barbara is officially an oldie, that'll teach yer xx

Pamela L. What classifies an oldie in your world? Very oldie!!!!

Diana M. It was a faded maroon in the 60's. My Dad used to say, with a grin on his face, they should add pale bule stripes to brighten it up....he was a Villa supporter(claret & blue).

Bryan D. Phew! I'm still a step away from losing my memory! So, they were painted maroon in the LMS/early BR days and green in the 1970s.

David M. Sorry about this but I don't recall any colour in the late 40's / 50's I thought they were just a dirty grey as in unpainted or creosoted wood !

Elaine H. Younger! Me! How kind! Still disagree about Maroon. How about you Terry?

Chris G. Looks like the entrance to Steptoe's yard.

Elizabeth M. I don't remember them with any colour, just a set of dirty old gates.

Helen J. I can't remember the gates being any particular colour - probably a well worn black shall I say. My Mum used to work on the fish stall when i was young and I was given a half pint of cockles (in a glass pot) while I was in the pram to keep me amused while Mum worked. I do actually remember this in distant memory though - i was probably coming up to the age of 2(ish).

Brian E. I seem to recall a brown sort of purple. The Radcliffe St. gates to the Queen Vic. yard were blue.

Heather L. I remember going there when I was a toddler !

Terry L. If I recall correctly, there was a cobbled lay-by in front of the Markets wall (Roadside)

Penny G. I always remember the gates being a brown colour and the ones round the corner Glyn street side!

Ken C. Helen, do you realise he was your uncle Frank? I think your fathers 2nd oldest brother after John. I think they went to Canada after the 1st world war..

Terry L. The Rolls of cloth I carried through them gates for Mr G Sweet.

Ruth E. Every Friday on Barleys stall dark & very cold xx

Pat G. Where would these gates have been - obviously before my time .

Bryan D. They fronted the Stratford Road. The wall has been pulled down, together with the northern wing of the building. What's left is the library and town meeting room. In the picture you can see the spire of the Wesleyan Chapel in the background.

Pat G. Thank you Bryan. When was the wall knocked down? I vaguely remember a market inside the building, before it moved to the Agora, but I really don't remember the gates.

Bryan D. I don't know when the wall and the buildings were knocked down Pat. For many years I did not set foot in Wolverton. Someone in this group will know. It. May have been around the time of the Tesco development or later.

Terry L. We had several arson attacks on the Market Hall in the early 80's, perhaps the wall was removed so it could be seen easily ?

Phillip W. It was way before Tesco. It must have come down in the 70's.

June L. Love it Bryan, enjoyed my Friday shopping with my mum in there.

Sandra and Steve A. What memories come flooding back, Mum made the best fish and chips with fresh fish from the market. I remember the fishmonger told us that he used to rub ice into his hands to keep them warm one the cold mornings. This is Wolverton to me, happy, safe and neighbourly times.

Linda Ann J. Lovely memories.

Janet S. I used to love to go to Lawson stall to spend my pocket money, while my mum was choosing material from sweets stall to make my sister and I summer dresses.

Will H. As someone who moved to the area in 95 I had no idea at all that there was a market in that location.

Gareth G. In my day I recall those gates as being brown. Passed through them many times often on an errand for my dad to get his regular pint of cockles and winkles from that very same fish stall. Always loved the atmosphere around the market as a young boy.

Inside the Market Hall

Geoff Ll. Thanks for all the comments. Just like so many of you I can smell the place and hear the hustle and bustle. One of my favourite stalls was the seed merchants, I think called Britains, and many of the seeds were sold loose. Winkles on a Friday from the fish stall and the toys, often looked at in envy by a young boy. My three Great Aunts kept a shop in Bradwell but on a Friday they brought a case full of wares and had a stall in the Market Hall.

Market hall interior 1980

Chris G. Used to have a big model of a smiling pigs head in the middle of Harry Browns didn't they?

Donna S. I remember the pigs head... and the smells of the place..

Jill G. Yep can smell it, fish meat and cheese yuk but still nostalgic :)

Brian E. Yes Chris, the smiling pig's head, around which was a banner reading,' pleased to meet you, meat to please you.'

Pamela J. We had the Queens coronation party in the old market hall.

Ian H. Great stuff Geoff

Ruth E. Best Chitlings in town from Browns.

Vivienne B. Mum used to buy our meat there, lovely old picture.

Bryan D. This could be the north eastern wing. Any thoughts?

Brian E. I will say, upstairs, those windows overlooking Church Street?

Bryan D. The school/market hall was on higher ground than the other side of Creed St, so the view from the window would pick out the Creed St. roofline.

John R. The best pork pies, sausage rolls,and fagots. They personified the fact that nothing on a pig would go to waste. They had all sorts of pork "meats" that were really very tasty, I just can't remember what they were all called.

Vivienne B. We use to have Faggot on a Friday, wouldn't dream of eating it know though Lol

Susan B. I liked his pork pies, some of my christmas mornings I would ask for pork pie for breakfast which was a treat any other time of the year I wouldn't be able too

Margaret C. I loved the pork dripping on toast.

Ian H. Especially the brown jelly at the bottom of the dripping Margaret. Not forgetting with a little bit of salt and pepper eh??

Susan B. Remember having that as a child Margaret, I did like the brown Jelly the best

Pam F. Brawn was one John.

Vivienne B. We use to like dripping on bread(think of the calories) Didn't they use to do paste (pate) when they had weighed it, it was wrapped in grease proof paper then put in a paper bag

Ruth E. My staple diet as a child dripping on toast. Mmm.

Pam F. yes they did. x

Margaret C. and the paste had a thick yellow topping..fat i expect..

Pam F. See what you've all done, i'm yearning dripping on toast. We used to toast the bread in front of the coal fire. Gorgeous.

Susan B. I wonder if it taste the same which you can buy in the supermarket these days

Margaret C. Enjoy the trip down memory lane am feeling tad rough so of to bed..All having fireworks enjoy and stay safe....x

Pam F. No nothing does. They used to sell bacon and when you fried it the fat was all crispy and lovely. Goes all watery now!!! :-((

Susan B. Sorry to hear this Margaret, hope you feel better soon

Pam F. One day at a time Margaret take care x

Andrew C. On Fridays after I had done my morning paper round I pushed a barrow full of toys and games down there for Lawsons.

Terry L. I used to sit with an old boy called Jacky from Stony, on a Friday he would always get Chittlings from the market and sit eating them when he got back a lunch time, always confused me because I am sure he was of Jewish stock !

Alan C. In 1958(I think I have the year right) before the then new Radcliffe School was built we had our Friday classes at the Church Institute, we went at lunch time to the Market and got some winkles and using a bent pin we would eat at the back of the class.

The Market Hall on Creed Street

When the Railway Works Ruled

The Railway Works still employed thousands in the 1960s, although the decline had already started. The following pictures of the "rush hours" give some flavour of the period.

Angela C. I remember the whistle going and every one coming out the gate @ 12 0 clock

Gloria S. I remember the works whistle. 12.25 then 1.25 pm.

Angela C. sorry I got the time wrong it went as I left infant school so thought it was 12 lol x

Chris G. Is that Harry Lime leaning up against the gate post?

Mark B. Oh Halcyon days, the only problem was getting knocked flying in the rush, it was even worse at home time at 4.30! Bike, cars, motor bikes and very fast moving men!

Pete B. That's the most energy these guys would use in a day . they would never move that fast once clocked in

David M. Another iconic photograph of the Wolverton of our childhood

Sue R. What a wonderful photo.

Margaret Ck. Happy Days!!

Susan B. Many days I use to go and wait outside these gates waiting for my dad to come out in the afternoon.

Tracy S. When we lived with my grandparents for a while at the North Western, I can remember sitting at the lounge window watching all the workers come out of work. It was like a sea of

Lunchtime at works

people when the siren went off.

Pamela L. Thanks for a super photo It always amazed me that the men from Stony Stratford and Bradwell managed to go home for lunch. My Dad used to walk to Gloucester Road and back could not have had much time to sit down and eat.

Jackie N. That's exactly as I remember it.....what a great photo!!

Molly H. So did my Dad Pam.

Sarah T. Brilliant photo my grandpa came home every lunch time and my gran would have his dinner ready, I would run to meet him down the jitty lovely memories xxx

Edith H. Pam my Dad used to cycle home to Gloucester Road for lunch. Up, what to me seemed, a very steep hill. I also remember the cart loads of wood. Used to get a lift on top of the wood. Cant remember where I got on the cart though. Don't think it was right down at the front.

Pat H. My dad used to cycle home to Bradwell for dinner then after the 1 o'clock news go back again. Like Edith I used love to ride in the wood truck offering rides to my friends to go back up the hill.

Janet B. I think as children we all used to have a ride in the wood trucks being taken back . It was good fun emptying and stacking the wood. Had to watch out for splinters though !!

Adrian C. Lovely photo.

Rod H. We used to get paid a shilling to help the men with wood trucks down the hill, unload the truck, & then take the truck back for them.

Pat B. Could that be Dick Henson used to live in Bedford st. In

19

the overcoat on the right behind the bike?

Brian J. I thought that was him as well Pat.

Anne S. Yes Pat it is. I couldn't remember his name but we lived in the same street. Lovely man.

Pat B. He re-covered a chair for us once.

Lorraine B. That's the gate my Dad and Grandad used to come out of when the works whistle went at lunch times, school used to finish at the same time and we'd all meet up at home for a lovely hot dinner that mum had cooked.

Pat B. Can't see your Dad Lorraine. I've looked under the hats but he is not there.

Lorraine B. He was probably first out and already home eating my mum's bacon and onion clanger!

Going home

Pete B. WHOO HOO, MY FIRST MOPED ON THE ROAD . NSU QUICKLY, bought from Flemings in stony stratford for £5 in nov 1972 . I road it miles illegally till my 16th birthday in Feb 73 when I got my Yamaha

Chris G. Yep certainly looks like Dave H, cap on ready to do the fire stuff after hours maybe?

Jennifer T. Fab pics.

Sharon F. Great photos

Mike B. The initials on the Fire Station - 'LN&SR', 'LW&SR' or other?

David Wd. LM&SR. London, Midland and Scottish Railway.

Lorraine B. Lorna Bone, is that your dad pushing his bike through the gate, with his buddy Walt Stephenson just ahead of him?

Tracy S. Definitely looks like Walt.

Lorna B. I think it is and it definitely looks like Walt. I'm seeing Dad later so I'll try and show him.

Chris G. I thought it was Walt to originally but there was a very similar chap worked down that end of the Works that wore glasses, I think that's him. Could be a relation maybe, can't for the life of me remember his name though.

Pauline D. Love these old photo's

Martin G. I think the man on the moped might be Harry Hunt from Stony,I know he worked for BR at Wolverton.The chap pushing the bike in front of the van is John ??????,his nickname was Wink,also from Stony.

Chris G. Ignore the above, looking at the pic on my phone it looked like the possible Walt was wearing glasses, that could well be him.

Terry L. Yep definitely Walt !!

Terry L. Bryan, were all these pic's taken in 1968 ?

Bryan D. More likely 1967 as I was living and working in Manchester from September of that year.

Terry L. Fantastic, look forward to picking more faces out.

Chris G. Looks like Doug Nicholls directly behind the car?

Terry L. I think Walt had the same bike for 30 plus years.

Chris G. Still goes out on it (or one similar) now, puts a lot of us younger ones to shame.

Terry L. The man pushing the bike in front of the Bedford truck I initially thought was Mr Gerald Hobson, but now I can see it is a man whose name escapes me from Stony an avid Stony Stratford FC supporter, my Dad Peter Levitt will know. is it Brown ?

David Wd. Terry, the name I was thinking of for the man pushing bike in front of the Bedford truck, is John Grimsley!

Terry L. Yep my Dad has confirmed Wink Grimsley, Sparky in the works.

Terry L. He'll be on here later and might put a few names to faces. that's me Dad not Wink!

Lorraine B. Definitely John (Wink) Grimsley pushing his bike in front of the van, he was in the same class at Stratford school as my dad (Colin Willett).

Martin G. John Grimsley......thats it Terry!! Talking of Stony football Terry, do you remember the likes of Dick Ellis and Cyril Stimson?

Peter L. I can see why you may think the man on the moped may be Harry Hunt but definitely not him. He worked at Druces in 1968 and I don't think Harry ever had any wheels.

Terry L. No Martin, but My Dad will maybe !

Martin G. Is that Harry Snr or Harry Jnr, Pete?

Peter L. Harry is around 76 now, was his dad's name Harry as well?

Martin G. Yes.I think it was Harry Snr.

Martin G. Still see Harry Jnr,he lives near me in Stony.

Brian J. Certainly looks like our Walt followed by it looks like frank Williams.

June L. I can see Wink there with his bike.

Outside Muscutt & Tompkins

Muscutt and Tompkins: Newspapers and Tobacco

Pete B. I was a butchers boy next door at Baxters butchers .

Tim H. The collecting box outside is from a different era as well.

Derek W. Is that Allan Wills ?? and **Pete B.** were you at Baxters during David Snow's reign?

Bryan D. David worked at the shop on the Square Derek. It certainly looks like Alan, although I though he wore glasses.

Derek W. He may have done Bryan, but definitely managed Baxters in Stratford Rd before moving on. Alan only wore reading glasses IFRC

Gill B. You are right Derek, David was manager at the Stratford Rd Baxters. Fred Griffiths was Manager on The Square.

Brian J. Des Chilton coming out of shop, that looks like Archie Wilkinson just going in I think, need a second opinion Wolvertonians

Bryan D. I guess I missed that Gill. I obviously remember him working with Fred on the Square and then I thought he had moved on to Pianoforte Supplies, but plainly he did a stint at the Stratford Road in between.

Derrick S. I would have said Archie Wilkinson going into the shop. He lived at the top of Radcliffe Street.

Tracy W. OMG I remember that shop dad bought my comics from there wow memory ...

Ian H. Well spotted Brian that is Archie!

Rod H. As kids we used to pick rose hips & sell them to M & T for a shilling a large bag, they used to make rose hip syrup & sell it.

Pete B. Fred Griffiths was a lovely bloke. I thought it was Derek snow not David.

Derek W. Re Fred Griffiths Pete Beale, I knew him well and remember he worked in Budgens?? in Stony after finishing butchering. Believe his wife name was Pauline.

Brian J. Cigs machine outside the shop, that wouldn't have lasted long nowadays.!!

Martin G. Nor the charity box Brian

Andy M. Nor the bike!!

Martin G. Thats true Andy. Did Fred Griffiths ever work for the Co-op butchers in Wolverton.........I seem to remember the name when I used deliver meat from Wolverton to Stony?

Barbara E. I worked in Muscutt & Tompkins on Saturday's in the early 1970's.

Colin T. Fred Griffiths ran Baxters Butchers on the Square Wolverton.

Ian H. Get Archie's cycle clips!

Ian H. and the paper-boy saying"stuff the paper round!!!"

Mark B. I worked at M & T delivering papers in Wolverton, selling papers (the chronicle an echo) at the works middle gate and the papers at the Station on some mornings. It was great but hard work all for £ 2.50 a week in the late 70,s

Anne S. I think Mrs Bowler (from Haversham) & Mrs Copas (from New Bradwell) worked in M & T.

Anne S. My brothers & I also had paper rounds 65-70.

Jackie N. I delivered magazines and the Wolverton Express from here in the early 60s-oooh, staggering in there at 6.30 in the morning! Then home to scrambled egg on toast before setting off to the Radcliffe......

Margaret Ck. Mary Shouler (Dillow) from Old Bradwell worked in there too.

Barbara E. Delivered morning papers early mornings early 70's

Mark B. I sure I remember the two Eileen's that worked there in the mornings, one from Bradwell.

Barbara E. Lots of names keep coming up that I remember

Brian E. What a wonderful picture. The "Spastic Girl" collecting box, and the cigarette machine on the wall.

Pat H. One was Eileen Copas from Glyn St; she ran Wolverton cubs.

Shirley B. Aunt Gladys and Uncle Ralph owned that shop. Well they were my dads cousins but we had to call them Aunt and Uncle. I believe john the son is still living in Wolverton.

David Wn. Bryan ,we both worked there as paperboys from 1954 -1959. Ar one time I had both morning and evening rounds. Earned £1.00 a week (£20 in current money). Remember Mr Ralph? Seemed a pretty miserable bloke at the time.He gave me a glowing reference for my first job at Unilever. I used to go with Reg in the van and pick up the Star ,Standard and Evening News from the railway station.

Bryan D. Proceeds of which David bought us our bikes, photographic materials from Dales and (also from Dales) chemicals to try and make gunpowder in your Dad's shed. Ralph Tompkins always struck me as a highly anxious type, always living on his nerve ends. His wife ran the stationery shop at Number 9. Reg Tomlin, who I believe was married to Ralph's sister Joyce, was a more genial character. sadly he died at a youngish age. He used to help in the newsagents at high peak periods in the mornings and evenings and then run the printing press during the day. The morning paper round rate was 13/6 and the evening round 6/6d. The evening round was harder work for less money I always thought. I did however sell the Chronicle and Echo at the Works gate by the station.

Pat H. Just had a thought and had to stop ironing. I think the other Eileen was Eileen Tuckey also from Bradwell, she was the wife of Sam the butcher. I think her maiden name was Glenn. Ah well back to work.

Shirley B. Our dad did the paper round to the out laying villages. they gave him the job because he could drive. that was 1938 ish.

Susan B. I done all the three newsagents on paper rounds and done one with my uncle on a Sunday too.

Barrie H. I had 3 paper rounds with Lawsons.

Alan C. Bryan are you sure the rate for the morning round was 13/6 I had the Stratford Road Anson road route from 1958 to 1962 and thought I only got 9/6d.

Jackie N. I got 10 shillings (50 p!) -for delivering magazines all week (and they were spread all over Wolverton -big gaps between each "drop") and Wolverton Express to half of Wolverton on Friday, which, as everyone had a copy ,meant that I had to go back to the shop a couple of times as I couldn't carry them all at once.......

Bryan D. At this distance in time Alan I wouldn't swear on a stack of bibles that it was, but these figures have lodged themselves in my mind: my first round doing Old Wolverton paid me 8/6d, then I got a main round in Wolverton for 11/6d which increased to 13/6d before I "retired". Perhaps others can contribute their memories.

Dave A. and wore ties...

Janet B. In 1952 I delivered magazines and the Wolverton Express. Like you Jackie so many W.E. took me ages to deliver, all for the princely sum of five shillings. [25p]

Bryan D. Delivering magazines, what Ralph Tompkins called "The Book Round" was always the hardest. On the other hand it was only once or twice a week was it not? The Radio Times featured prominently - almost everyone took it.

Janet B. I delivered magazines Tuesday to Thursday.Wolverton Express early Friday morning.

Harvey A. I must have missed out here. My recollection is that the morning paper round in the mid 1950s was 1/6d and magazines were 1/- per round. The morning paper round earned more because the papers weren't marked with the address, we had to learn the round; as we also had to take on board any temporary or permanent adjustments (horrendous during works holiday fortnight). My morning paper round went up Cambridge Street and down the old part of Windsor Street . Furze Way was added at some stage. On Saturdays we also had to go round collecting money from those who elected not pay in the shop.

Derek W. I used to do a paper round at Bradwell for "Wagger" Watts. Was paid 8 shillings a week and remember one house in

Bradwell Road opposite the Co-op had a Telegraph and Daily Worker (The communist paper at the time), quite a contrast.

Harvey A. Yes Janet, you have reminded me, Tuesday to Thursday were the main magazine days. On Tuesday the main titles were Womans Weekly and to a lesser extent, Womans Realm, and on Thursday as well as the Radio Times, there were Woman and Woman's Own. That bag on a Thursday must have been heavy! Comics featured quite well too but were more spread through the week. I don't remember any magazines on a Monday but thought there were a few on Fridays. But then Friday was Buster day (I've got no idea how the W/E got that nickname). I was working at BBC Publications in the early 1970s. The then editor was a chap called Geoffrey Channon I think. He saw the title of Radio Times as not relevant in a television age and tried to change it by first making the title RT (for Radio Television I guess), but public opinion forced him to change his mind and it reverted to the archaic title we still have (though it is no longer a BBC publication)

Bryan D. You've probably nailed it Harvey. I was guilty of some inflation. It was, as you say, 1/6d for a newspaper round and with the 'collecting round" on Saturday after everyone had woken up that gave us 10/6d. per week. I am sure we got a pay increase at some point but now I am unsure of the amount.

Harvey A. Yes Bryan, I am sure this happened. I do remember agitating for an increase but nothing transpired even though I had direct access to the boss man! However he probably felt a bit of pride in me being 'union minded', for dad was very much involved with NUVB (Vehicle Builders) when he was at the Works.

Alan C. I agree I think I got the 10/6 after an increase I do know that when I retired and went to Lloyds Bank in 1962 my monthly salary cheques were less that £30, and I have never had so much free spending money since, mind you a pint of Wells was only 10p at the Craufurd

David M. I seem to remember getting 7/6d a week for my grocery round for Mitchells of Green Lane. The worse one of the week was a delivery to Bradville... that bloody hill up over the canal was a real killer with a great box of groceries on the front and no gears ! That one always gave a good tip though!

Brian E. That ruddy canal bridge hill at Bradwell is still a killer for me today!

Alan C. Before there was a swimming pool at Wolverton used to bike over to Newport to go swimming and training in their outdoor pool that was always freezing cold!!! and going up the hill at the Canal at the Black horse was always tough,and the Station Hill was no fun either.

Harvey A. Ouch, David, I feel for you even at this distance. Somewhere about 1956 Oscar Tapper, then a teacher at WGS, got us involved in an archaeological dig near the A5 the other side of Denbigh Bridge. I used to bike up and over that bridge on the way to Loughton (and then to the A5), and that hill was torment even without a heavy grocery box

Bryan D. Oscar Tapper! What a great character Harvey! Old tweed jacket with elbow patches, curly collar, unpressed trousers. He lived on a canal boat at Fenny when he first turned up in 1954. I too worked on the Magiovintum site which was actually south of Fenny Stratford, so an even further bike ride. I even turned up a Roman coin, which at the time I found very exciting.

Harvey A. Yes Bryan, all sorts of stories abound about Oscar T, though a group of us were entertained by him to tea (of sorts) on his canal boat one day. There was also a rumour that his barge had sunk on one occasion but this is probably a figment of schoolboy imagination. I do however feel that he admitted to us on one occasion that if he was thumbing a life to school from Fenny (which he did, much I think to Mr Morgan's frustration and embarrassment that one of his staff should do such a thing), he would, if no lift came along, lie down in the road in order to make a car stop!

Bryan D. Christine Metcalfe once told me a story about herself, Harry Johnson and OT going down to Swains one day to buy a shoelace. OT had broken a shoelace that morning. Anyway Mr Wilcox got out a pair of shoelaces for him but OT said, "But I only need one." And, in Christine's own words 'the poor man' duly split open the packet and sold him one shoelace. This cracked her up.

Brian E. I was seated at Tescos this afternoon, looking across the road at Muscott & Tompkins. I could not for the life of me figure out which wall that cigarette machine was affixed to. Where the man is standing there is no doorway?

Bryan D. I've just taken a look at Google Street View Brian. It does make sense. The old lock up M&T shop, now Smart Move, has a new front with the door in the middle. The door to the right, which used to lead upstairs over Lampitts/Darling and Wood is also still there, but somewhat modified.

The AGORA and All That

The Agora became the next phase of redevelopment, demolishing a good section of Wolverton built in the 1860s and 1870s. It was the result of an effort by Milton Keynes Development Corporation to provide an amenity for Wolverton. The intention was to build a covered market place which could also be used as a leisure facility. The roller skating rink as popular but it eventually lost its popularity and the building went into decline. Justified or not, the Agora became for many a symbol and a cause of Wolverton's later problems and some of these views are reflected here. As we write there are plans to demolish the building, open up Radcliffe Street once more, and restore residences to the area.

Not much of a photographic record survives of the parts of Church Street and Buckingham Street that were pulled down for the new development. Possibly the south side of Church Street was rarely photographed because the camera lens was forced to face the sun. Here are some pictures and comments.

Chris G. I remember watching it go up as a 14 year old thinking, corrrrrrrr, this is going to be brilliant...
Steve A. And for a while it was Chris, but not long.
Chris G. Indeed. I remember someone making up the rumour that there was a crease in the plans and they'd put it in the wrong way round. Very soon people were telling you that that was fact. Some people no doubt think it to this day.
Steve A. Yes Chris that's right! That's supposed to be why it's at

Agora under construction

an angle to the other streets.

Jane B. I heard that too - so it's not true then? Jeez, me being gullible YET AGAIN !!!!

Chris G. People will also tell you 'they' burnt down the Science and Arts for its car park, forgetting it happened a few years before this was even planned.

Alan Cr. Hoax.

Peter A. Originally thought it was gonna be an indoor pool but they came up with that stupid idea earlier this year. The Science & Arts still stood although a partially burnt out shell and was demolished to make way for the car park.

Peter A. I remember this shop it used to have in the window a small Chinese lantern I was obviously taken by it for me to have that memory still.

Graham T. It was owned/occupied by a Mrs Nichols for many years.The window[just behind the little boy]had a board in it to advertised anything you wished to sell--it cost sixpence to put a notice in.

Peter A. Was a bit of a junk shop.

Buckingham Street -Radcliffe Street Corner

Jackie N. I'd forgotten all about this,but recognised it straight away!

Valerie D. Remember this shop very well

Aimée M. Where is this? Cambridge street

Bryan D. It's the corner of Buckingham St and Radcliffe St. The Agora is there now.

Aimée M. Oh ok thanks

David M. Same as you Jackie I had forgotten it too ... but recognised it straight away

Ant K. Who is the little boy ?

Janet B. At the bottom of the garden was a shed , which was in the back way of Buckingham St. Used to take shoes there to be repaired.

Jackie N. Oh, I'd forgotten him too-a real cobbler-used to hold the nails/tacks in a row in his mouth while he was talking!

Toni B. I recalled it right away too. But it was hidden well back in my mind.

Bryan D. Here's a view which hasn't been seen in Wolverton for over 30 years. The Agora usurped its place.

This was Eady the Butcher on the south east corner of Radcliffe Street. At the time of this drawing they were into the third generation of butchering in Wolverton.

Pete B. remember looking through the windows as a kid, it must have closed in the early 60s

Hazel S. Bryan, where was Anstey's Record and Sheet Music Shop?

Philip E. We lived here when we were first married the co op bought it from Mrs Eady. Happy times. Anstys was next to the two houses not the co op..

David Wd. I think I am correct in saying that the shop front from "Eady's", is at the museum, being used as the front of the Ironmongers.

Philip E. The window going up the side from the main shop

Gas showroom, Buckingham Street

View to North of Square

View after clearance

Eady's Butcher Shop

window.

Elaine C. I worked in King's Bakery. Tragically demolished for the Agora. Haven't tasted bread quite like it since.

Janet B. Anstey's had two steps and the side window was slanting. the Co.op then had the shop, selling and renting TVs..

Phillip W. Nice to see what Wolverton was like before the eye sore.

Bryan D. I'm on the other corner now. This is King's Bakery as I remember it before they extended the front in the 70s. There must have been a sign, maybe a Hovis sign, but I can't recall its appearance or placement. Any thoughts?

John R. I remember the Hovis sign being on the Radcliffe Street side wall

Bryan D. Thanks John. That's right.

Pam F. Love this picture.

Ant K. I am almost certain there was an Hovis sign on the front. But also I think there was a sign on Radcliffe Street. I thought the left window was a bay window also, but not sure. Better have a family pow wow ! Great picture though. All I remember is that you had to climb a few steps to the shop. The pavement was elevated at that point

Bryan D. Thanks Ant. I was rather hoping you would catch this picture. Please get back to me.

Hazel S. Jim seems to remember the 'Daren Bread' and 'Hovis'

Kings Bakery c. 1960

specialist brown loaf signs appearing on the shop front.

Pam F. I think it may have been a bay window, I did think there were more steps up and maybe further back but then I may remember it with a child's eyes. Still love it though, well done.

Martin G. Brings back memories.............buying bread rolls on the way home from Moon Street and eating them at the bus stop waiting for the 392 to Stony.

John R. To make this the perfect picture, you need to incorporate the wonderful smell that came out of the bakery.

Dave A. 391 or 392 ? 392 all round the houses...I remember a 392 turning up Marina Drive one day - the driver hadn't quite mastered the route.

Gareth G. As I remember there was a green and gold Hovis sign on the front over the entrance. I was in there every other day for a large tin loaf and a Hovis, if I had 3d I could get a tiny little hovis loaf all to myself, anyone remember them? The smell of the place used to make my mouth water then unfortunately by the time I got home the tin loaf looked like a flock of starlings had been at it, had a few clip's round the ear for that!

Bryan D. I bet you could find an app that does just that John.

Graham T. To the right of the bakery was a wool and knitting patterns shop[can't remember the name];followed by a mens hairdressers.GT

Edith H. Graham it was Stricklands, see my comment above.

Graham T. Pam is quite right in regard to a greater number of

33

steps and a bay window to the left--also the concrete at the front had a slight slope rather than level.GT

Chris G. Barbers was Mr Garwood

Graham T. I vaguely remember the Hovis sign being in the blank window above the door.GT

David Wn. The bakery was set back from the pavement with a sloping concrete apron to some steps

Harvey A. For what it's worth I tend, (i.e. I could be wrong) to agree with Ant as regards the frontage, with Pam as far as a deeper step up and Hazel as to signage. As to Chris' point about the barbers, before Garwood it was Tom Farndon (until about 1958 I would think)

Graham T. Yes--the frontage was much deeper and I think there were three steps up ???.GT

Bryan D. Thank you all for your useful comments. I'll wait for Ant to get back on this and will then do a revised version.

Ant K. Yes there were more steps. And a Hovis sign. I think my uncle n aunt actually have a photo. Sadly I have nothing other than an oil painting which was of the shop just before it was knocked down. Done by one of our customers I believe ! A wonderful gesture at time of grief.

Bryan D. If you are able to put up a photo of the oil painting, or perhaps the other photo I would appreciate it Ant. Until it was so rudely taken away from your family it was the oldest surviving bakery in Wolverton. It was built in 1860 as a purpose-built bak... See More

Susan B. Brilliant picture.I can smell the bread cooking now, great shop, it was sadly missed when they closed it

Sue T. Would be great to have a drawing of my Dads shop (Garwoods the Hairdressers) I only remember the Kings in the photo posted by Phil James, and not Bryan D.s fabulous drawing

Bryan D. I do plan to reconstruct Church St from photos (where available) and memory, so your Dad's shop and Stricklands will be on the list. However I have another project which I have to finish first, so it may be a while. I remember when your Dad came to Wolverton and took over the shop. He also sold Astra fireworks. He ran a Fireworks Club so that you could contribute a shilling or so a week to save up for the week of Nove 5th when he was allowed to sell them.

Sue T. What a lovely memory, will remind him of that when I see him tomorrow

Jackie N. Radcliffe Street 1975.

Tracey W. Don't know whether I'm right but when I was a kid I think that little building was a coal place mum used to go in and pay for coal.

Susan B. Then the dreaded Agora came along, nothing wrong the way Wolverton was, why couldn't it stay the way we all remember it

Julie C. What's the shop that is now the bank on the corner?

Pina R. It's the Anglia Building Society as was....

Chris G. And the yellow hut was Dave Lovelands bookies.

Pina R. Wasn't Billingham's Chip shop a bit higher up on the other side of the alleyway? (so it would have been behind the Gas showroom)

Hazel S. At selected times, Ken Pitman, the Vet used to have a surgery here.

Anthony Z. Great photo , brings back lots of memories.

Bryan D. Great to see this. I see the Marler Hall has gone. Pina,

Kings under demolition 1975

Billinghams was on Creed Street. The Building Society went through several phases - all in the same location - Wolverton, Northampton, Anglia here, and now Nationwide.

Chris G. Only the fascia is Phil, the rest is old Victorian terrace.

Chris G. I've just noticed you can still make Dave Lovelands name out on the hut

Dale Becks Great to slip back to 1975 & a good time for music & my last year at the Radcliffe.xx

Chris G. Theres nothing new there at all Phil bar a lick of paint and the Anglia sign.

Dave Millard I still have my old Anglia pass book, my parents still get letters (from nationwide) it appears i have earned £5 in interest on the small amount that was left in there in 1978. so no retiring yet unfortunately

Bryan D. Take a second look Chris. I would say that block has been significantly re-built.

Chris G. Apologies, we're talking at cross purposes, I'm talking building in that picture, not whats there now.

Bryan D. Sorry, I now see your comment in context.

Jackie N. Re: taking these sort of photos.... my Dad was a great photographer and very interested in local history too. When this was taken everyone obviously knew what was happening and he decided to record events . I bet at the time people thought "why is that bloke taking pictures of half demolished buildings?" Very forward thinking was my Dad-just wish he was here to join in with us -he would be dead chuffed!

Chris G. Even in these days of digital when you can rattle of a couple of hundred shots in a couple of minutes we still tend to overlook shots like this so fair play to your Dad Jackie.

Pina R. Bryan, I'm sure that there used to be a chip shop there when I was younger, maybe it wasn't Billinghams but it was after Creed St closed...

Chris G. There was one for a while the other side of Church St to where the one is now wasn't there? Or is this another one Pina?

Pina R. That was Gregory's Chris before they moved across the road. I'm thinking there was one behind the Gas showroom right by Buckingham St back alley, would have been opposite the bookies.....don't know why I seem to have a memory of one being there......I'll have to get in touch with chippy Lee & ask him if he remembers!

Maria Miceli He's in Wolverton at the mo.

Pina R. Ask him when you talk to him Maria!! x

Maria Miceli Will do!

Pam B. The old building there was used by the vet on a Saturday morning. I use to help him when i was about 13.

Pam B. At one time it was a bookies my dad use to bet there.

John H. Pina R. , are you thinking of the wet fish shop along Church St.

Pina R. Nope! It was along this road.......beginning to think I dreamt it now!!

Janet B. The Co op had a veg and fish shop at the top of the square Pina but that would have been well before your time .

Bryan D. Check this out Pina. This was Billingham's Fish & Chip shop. Is that the one you were thinking of? http://www.facebook. com/photo.php...

Graham T. The shop that can be seen with the glass window, was, for a period a bookmakers.

Chris G. Yep see above comments Graham, Dave Lovelands

Pina R. That''s not the one I was thinking of @Bryan ....Will delve into my memory cells!!

Pina R. @Janet B. , I can remember the Co_op grocers, drapers & bank being on the Square. The drapers had a wooden staircase in it if I remember rightly. Didn't they sell the school blazers in there?

Bryan D. Good luck with that. The only chippie I can think of that remotely resembled your description was on Peel Road.

Maria M. OH pooh! Dad phoned and I forgot to ask him about that! Pina R.

Janet B. Yes you are correct Pina with all of the Co op shops. The shoe shop was next to the Drapery. The fruit and vegetable/ wet fish shop was on the corner of Aylesbury St and Radcliffe St .

Ian H. The chippy in Peel Road was Smith and Larners I think. They used whale fat at one time when cooking fat was scarce.

Pina R. I can remember the one on Peel Rd!

David M. Often used to queue on a Friday night at the Peel Road Chippy -long double queue with a rail down the middle. It was quite a cabaret in there. My memory is probably playing me tricks (again) but I recall Mr Smith looking rather like Eric Morecambe. Good fun whilst I was waiting for the fish and chips and hoping there were some scratchings left

Ian H. Mr Smith certainly had very dark hair David, I think he was quite short but stocky?

David M. Thats right he was , but definitely a bit of a comedian

Ian H. I remember that wooden barrier so well David and when I do I think of scratchings and salt pots and vinegar and threepenny bits!!

Ian H. Do you remember when he scooped the chips up from the boiling fat in a big square metal sieve ,tested the chips with his fingers and if they were ready he bashed the sieve once or twice against the fryer then lofted the chips into the open tray on the side!! I can see it now and guess what we're having chips for dinner today

Ian H. I may have mentioned it before but just in case.............. Mr Larner was the gentleman who came to Wolverton with his trailer that sold wet fish.

Janet B. Used to play games outside ,while we waited for the shop to open. In those days games featured around film stars , if my memory is correct .

Ian H. Ingrid Bergman or Betty Gable for you Janet ?

Janet B. Both Ian! loved to go to the Palace on a Saturday afternoon. cant remember the Empire having matinees. Still like to go to a good film.

Ian H. The Empire did as well mate, I spent so much time in the flicks to the detriment of my education!! The last time I went into a cinema was in Telford when "A Fish Called Wanda" was showing ....over twenty years ago!!

Janet B. You've missed some good ones then! Also some rubbish.

David M. My abiding memory of the Empire was seeing a particularly dire film (can't even remember the title). On of the characters on screen uttered the line "My God this is dreadful". Then a voice like a foghorn somewhere near the back roared out "Yes and it's not getting any bloody better." Brought the house down that did.

Nick C. Talking of Kings the Bakers........Mr King putting loaves in oven, and Mr. Odell in foreground.

Vivienne B. This picture brings back so many memories

Susan B. Smell that bread thats just been cooked

Terry L. Mmmm!! Looks like John Le Mes

Ruth E. Oh Wow .....

Pat C. Were there O'Dells had a pub or guest house on main road not too far from cinema? I can remember a Jane O'Dell. Or Odell 1950's

Ian H. The Crauford Pat

Terry L. WHERE ?

Pat C. Thanks Ian didn't realise it was Crauford, think Jane went into the Prison Service. Seems to have changed a lot since my day Terry.

Ian H. So did my wife for many years Pat in many prisons! Not bad to be in the HMP and French ! Vive l'Europe

Bryan D. Wally Odell had the Craufurd. ex Tottenham Hotspur player I believe.

Ian H. When she was at the "Scrubs" Mad Mitchell escaped and

Mr King and Alf Nash at the Bakery

went through her back alley to get away!

Chris G. Phil, Grant or Peggy?

Ian H. On her last posting Featherstone, just outside Wolverhampton one of the locals said to her " ain't yow got a fooney accent! "

Elizabeth M. The chap at the front of this picture is Alfie Nash. He used to live in Bradwell Road, opposite the vicarage. My brother worked for Kings and him and Alfie used to do the Haversham run on a Wednesday afternoon. Alfie had a son (can't remember his name at the moment) and two daughters Margaret and Pauline. I went to school with the girls and they both live in Deanshanger now.

John H. The agora being built

Jane B. Gosh John - great pic!!! I'd forgotten what it looked like with all the other buildings still standing - why oh why was it inflicted on us - get rid of the damn thing!!!!!!

Peter W. Are there more pictures of its construction? Would be interesting to see.

Bryan D. Very interesting. So they still left some of those Church Street houses and shops in place while they built the Agora. Were they demolished later to make the car park?

Terry L. Yep Bryan, they may as well leave them alone for the amount of cars that park there...

Len E. I always try to park in my old living room :)

Andrew L. I was in Bushfield when it was being built and the teachers took us out to the Square occasionally to look. We were there at one attempt to lift the "record breaking" roof - when it

Church St and the newly constructed Agora

39

failed.

Stephen C. Worst thing they ever did building that.

Darren P. Hitting *like* isn't the word but quality pic!!

Constance O. We lived at 53 Church St, we had to move because they knocked it down, to build the Agora.

Andrew L. My last attempt at roller skating end badly on this ramp...

Heather F. Yes I remember this ramp my ended up with me breaking my arm twice but I would do it again loll

Hayley D. I remember this ramp well

Phillip W. Sooner this building is flattened the better it be for Wolverton.

Dave B. Why? To be replaced with flats or more take-a way's? Least as it stands there are options that will bring more people into town. Ok it could do with a cosmetic makeover :)

Brian E. No, not to be replaced by flats. To open up Radcliffe St & the Square and create an integrated town centre again, with bus stops, small shops and flower beds/tubs. To be replaced with something Wolverton wants & needs, not some architectural monstrosity foisted upon it by an overzealous and absent town-planner. There is no realistic way refurbishment can take place here.Bringing people into town is desirable, yes, but more important is making a town & community again for residents.

Dave B. I agree with you Brian as this paints a nice picture. It would open it all back up again, but the way housing is built now lol it will still look out of place :) Too be honest as a venue with potential for ideas, They could take it down and build something more desirable in another place in Wolverton, then still have the town opened back up. ☺

Roller Skating

Steve B. 23 years on and roller skating returns to The Agora tomorrow.....happy memories of Friday night's spring back to life!

Lynne P. Fell on my bottom when I went there ...so much fun ...good times...

Janice M. Have great memories from there! Glad to see it is finally going to be put to use.

Lynne P. I so miss the past ...it was fun ...innocent...and I would love to go there again.

Brian E. Yes, the dear, dead days beyond recall.

June L. Yes I agree with you Lynnette, I definitely wouldn't like to be a teenager these days, we were so innocent & naive & happy, I know I was. When I was going to move from Essex to Wolverton my work mates in London said be careful June, they are nearer to nature there, by golly they were Right.

I liked the simplicity of life then ,so complicated these days.

Karen A. Being in touch here with all the lovely photos and chat, helps to reach back xx

Ian H. I liked swinging on the small wooden gate at the front of our house, especially when the men from the works were coming home for their dinners.

Susan K. I went Roller skating at the Agora last night as did a number of IGUIW contributors.... and slipped right back into the

Roller Skating in the Agora

past!

June L. Did you enjoy it Susan?

Susan K. Brilliant fun June.

John H. Roller skating started in the Agora in the 70s. Anybody recognize these youngsters?

Heather F. No not me lol I was only just born in 1970 lol

Ron B. Is that CG in the skirt????

Stephen C. You could be right Ron. It was about this time he was a confused person.

Ron B. What do you mean was, Claz

John R. Is that Pete Crook in the background? Wouldn't surprise me, he's in half of the pictures posted in this group.

Chris G. No Ron that isn't Colin Gear, and nope not Pete either John.

David M. Took my daughter to the Agora for roller skating. Never forgave me for turning up to collect her one day whilst on my way to the Braddle tip (sorry - recycling centre) towing a trailer with an old toilet perched on it

Julie B. I think that is me in the skirt, with Frankie with the jumper around her waist but it would have been 79 or latter as I look about 10/11, well going by the haircut.

Terry L. I think this is the long awaited turning point for Wolverton and the Agora.

Mark B. That brings back some memories, is there a bar still up stairs and does it have the table top space invaders games?

Terry L. The Bar was still there this weekend!

Mark B. Is it open every weekend? I'm back down in mid-December.

Terry L. Yes, bring your skates!

Mark B. Cheers Terry, I'll bring my daughter for a go, may have a dabble myself again; been nearly 20+ years since I last had a go.

Richie B. Well the roller skating proved to be a success apparently over 500 through the doors. I can't walk today though.

Ruth E. I am going on Pensioners night with Richie B. Dad!

Richie B. So whose coming roller skating tonight then. Hope my hip holds out..lol...seeing as they aren't going to knock the building down any time soon soon. I think its good it's being used for the purpose it was built for..

Ron B. With your accident record. No thanks. lol

Craig T. Ooooooooooh yehhhhhhhhhh.........lol

Heather F. I wish I could but got to work lol

Jane B. I would Richie but I'm too old and creaky I'm afraid xxxx

Chris G. You want to take your old man in his chair for balance Richie, plus he'd enjoy the night out.

Richie B. I took Dad down that on Thursday. Nearly ended up in the shop at the bottom lol.

June L. Problem with walking but if someone is prepared to lift me on a pair of Rollers & give me a good shove, I'm game.

Ron B. Down that slope June.lol.xx

June L. I had better practice on my ramp then Ron xx

Steve B. Last time I put my skates on, I tested positive for WD40... was banned ever since!

Future of the Agora

Philip W. What do you think the chances are of the Agora being pulled down?

June L. Why have you heard anything then? Every one had to find alternate accommodation not to long ago because it was going to be pulled down, nothing happened!

Richie B. Can't see it my self not for a while any way !

John Rd. Ultimately the owners have to want it pulled down either that or sell it to someone who does. as much as we want it gone they cant be forced into it.

Phillip W. I have not yet hard anything about it but I am hoping it would.

Steve B. If they leave it long enough it will fall down all by itself!

Dale B. I think it just needs a Face Lift, just like a lot of us. A good place for Roller skating, years ago for some & having the crack with your mates, for others. I have noticed that some of the local business have moved over there to save on money on there Rental, shops, I imagine..!!

Agora from Square

John Rd. Who does roller skating now? would be better as a BMX or skate park but still its not viable to do so. knock it down and build new shops with flats above them. the company who owns it now would probably want around 3-5mil for that site, its massive including the car park so it would just get replaced with high density shop fronts/offices and flats.

Dorothy S. Sooner knocked down the better Wolverton people never wanted it built anyway it has been the start of WOLVERTON loosing the town's full value as a really decent town. Everything's been taken away now....

Dale B. Not to mention the British Rail Factory & all the workers on their Bikes, came flooding out at knock off time. Some would get straight home for their Tea, while others would stop off at the Crauford Arms, Where my Dad Tom would have the Beers lined up. Another thing I remember was the Radcliffe School Blazers & if you had the cheap dark red one, or the cherry Red. My first one was the Aubergine, from Fosters Men care & the lighter Cherry Red, came from the Co-op..!! Many a paper round you'd have to do & be able to help out with your earnings to get the one from the Co-op.Didn't matter too much though, as we would all write over each others in our last year there..!!

Len E.

Dale, I too had the maroon blazer and on the first day at Moon St I felt an outsider I hunted round for other pupils with the same coloured blazer as me. One other I remember is Mr Gee clapping eyes on me and saying "Oh no, not another Eccles" !!!

Linda K. John, roller skating is still very popular! Go along to Stantonbury Leisure Centre on a Sunday and you will find a packed roller skating session. People in MK just don't have anywhere regular to do it like they used to.

Much as I agree that the town was lovely in the pre-1979 days there is no going back to those days and I dread to think what would be built to replace the Agora. If anything at all. It could be left as wasteland. Surely it would be better to put some money into it and make it a useful building.

John Rd. But its not popular enough to warrant dedicated use of the Agora though. its all well doing it in a fully fledged leisure centre where they make money from other activities but I stand by my statement that the Agora is not viable for it anymore

Dale B. On that note, who remembers the Film Field of Dreams & the words, if you build it, they will come..? Well I believe anything is possible, with Wolverton & with the right Towns Committee to do the right thing & protect your Heritage. Next meeting to be arranged in a Pub of your choice, Ha!

Linda K. Everyone has brilliant ideas but they won't happen in the present climate. I am convinced that the powers that be would let Wolverton rot if they thought they could get away with it. Well, they have got away with it for years really. Terrible waste of a lovely town that would be cherished far more if it was in other parts of the country. In my opinion of course.

Colin T. THEY NEED TO PULL IT DOWN!

Linda K. So who do you think will build the new buildings and who are you expecting to occupy the shops within them?

John Rd. To be honest I don't think there is any need for more shop units within Wolverton, they is plenty enough already and if Tesco gets the go ahead to expand than then some of the current ones may turn empty anyways. Perhaps maybe that's why it has not already been ripped down. so we could end up with a few blocks of flats there....just careful what you wish for guys. not everyone will be pleased with what ever goes there

Sylvia A. Having worked in one of the office units in the agora for the last 11 years I can honestly say the agora is a dead centre...I do not for the life of me know how or why it survives...The actual Agora does NOT make any money...the small units downstairs are rented for ridiculous amounts of money but do no trade and never last for long. The offices upstairs well the main unit holders were MK college and the company I used to work for...now they're both gone. I have always said and still maintain that the Agora is used as a cover for something else...goodness knows what but it certainly isn't to make money. They have no substantial money coming in other than the lease from the Co-op. the other main traders were Colin and the pet shop who have also both gone now. So...where do you think there money is coming from to keep it open? Or do you also think there's something more to the agora than what we know? would be interested to know what others think.

John Rd. Well the old company who ran it went into administration a couple of years ago so I can only presume someone an investor possibly, must of bought the building off them and are biding their time to get their return on it

Sylvia A.
Yes it did go into administration and they did get a new purchaser although from what I heard they are connected to the previous owner!! Mr Mann who seems to be on a mission to take over the whole of Wolverton. The day it was supposed to go to auction under the administration order a "mystery" purchaser came forward. I know, I was there.

John Rd. A management buyout then. He probably bought the place for a pittance as well. Wise move by him to be honest as he could make a lot of money from the sale of it, but as I said in an earlier post, 3-5mil buying it and up to 10mil to develop it so to get a good return would require 4 or 5 story block with a big store for co-op/post office plus a couple smaller units then a shed load of residential an car parking. It will have to be a high density development

Linda K. Totally agree with all your posts Sylvia and John. But don't you think that a high density development would be no better than the Agora. The only thing that would look ok really would be housing that is similar to the Victorian ones (like up the other end of Church Street) or a grassed area/park which would at least open up to The Square. However I doubt either would provide the financial return that would be considered necessary.

Sylvia A. Mr Mann has always absolutely refused to sell which is why all the plans to knock it down and rebuild etc have never come to fruition. He refuses to sell it to the council. He could have made his money by selling it but money is not an issue for him when it comes to the agora which makes me think there's something else underneath it all. My opinion anyway.

Linda K. Think you are very probably right Sylvia. He has run that place into the ground. Must be for a reason.

Jane B. Well Sylvia - it would certainly explain WHY the bloody thing is still there - I think a lot of Wolverton residents have questioned just why it hasn't been demolished - but if there is an ulterior motive - well - there's our answer.

Sylvia A. I agree Linda, there was talk about knocking it down and building a new purpose built shopping centre in its place... but again it never happened nor will it ....they were also talking about reopening up the space to rebuild a road to link Church St with the square again...but again it seems that nothing will come to fruition and the building will just continue to fall into a state of total disrepair and be condemned.

Linda K. That sadly seems to be the story of Wolverton at the moment. The Vic opposite looks even sadder than the Agora. The town needs a benefactor! Not sure where it will find one though!

Sylvia A. Well guess who owns the Queen Vic. Last I heard it was owned by the same guy that owns the Agora, along with half the other properties in Church St.

Jane B. I just think it's really sad - here we are - on the World Wide Web - creating a little group that says we were proud to "Grow up in Wolverton" - and all around us the town we love is being gradually eroded away - maybe I'm just getting old but I just find it so sad

Sylvia A. I agree with you John, and sadly its the same wherever you go not just in MK..small towns are becoming badly neglected because the new modern large shopping centres are killing off the small independent shops and therefore the little towns will never be commercially profitable. so sad and very depressing.

John Rd. The council couldn't afford to buy and develop it plus whatever they would build there would be a lot worse than what anyone would build there. besides the council don't even build new homes anymore, they get things funded for them from essentially bungs from housing developers. as for a new purpose built shopping centre there is no point. it would fail as they are enough of them around in MK anyways plus we would never attract the big shops to little old Wolverton. look at the state of Fenny Stratford and Bletchley....do you really want a ghost town with poor shops like that in Wolverton?? I know I wouldn't. It's true Mr Mann owns the Vic. a friend of mine leases it from him. The place is a shambles an needs a lot of repairs which he won't pay out for.

Linda K. Didn't realise he owned the Vic. He is either on a one man mission to destroy Wolverton or he knows something that we don't and plans to make a financial killing one day. Funny how the places that he owns are in a state whereas other places like the Crauford and the Western seem to be doing OK.

John Rd. The Crauford does so well coz of the live music and its an award winning venue. the Western and Vic are mostly visited by the same piss heads to be honest. I always used to be in the latter 2 but soon got bored of them when I discovered the free party scene and most of the lads my ages seem to go to Stony or to the Wolverton town footy club these days.

Linda K. The people at the Crauford have done a great job. Shame there's no other decent pubs in Wolverton. The Vic used to be OK once.

John Rd. The Vic hasn't been any good since I was around 20 (5yrs ago) since then they have a few people run it one person lasted months. Another one of my mates Aunties had it for a bit but she used to let us get away with all sorts and she was ousted then someone else who didn't last long then the current person took over. Then there was a massive water leak which ruined the inside and it shut down for a while then my mate reopened it coz she couldn't get her money back for the lease. The Western has always been well run but its a bit of an old man's place now

Colin T. Good Evening Ladies & Gentlemen, It's been Fun reading you comments, Yes we all have our own idea's, I will not get into arguments over this Crap building, BUT Pull the thing down put the road back that was there in the first place for the good people of Wolverton, Amen .

Graham T. Agree with above--and the sooner the better.

An Architect's View

In 2010 Iqbal Alaam, who was a young architect in the 1970s working for MKDC reviewed many of the projects undertaken in the development of the new city. Here is his assessment of the Agora, which we have reprinted here with his permission. It is somewhat at variance with the views expressed above, but we reproduce it here for balance.

February 19, 2010

Wolverton, though only few miles away from Stony Stratford, is a very different town, almost in all respects. It is a historic Victorian Railway town, with a Milton Keynes like gridded housing core of terraces, surrounded by railway workshops.

The softness and rustic surroundings are nowhere to be seen and this shift in grain of the town was very sensitively picked up by the MKDC design team in designing this indoor market and Skating/Leisure Centre.

The shopping/leisure building had to be flexible in use and a large space framed covered area surrounded with two storey balcony/ circulation is housed in a robust engineering brick structure with references to Victorian brick decorations. The appearance and the architectural handling has been developed to provide a strong visual rhythm to accommodate 'uncontrolled' use and appearance, consequently the building is unlikely to win many beauty competitions but what a wonderful gift for a tough town this turned out to be.

It is refreshing and unusual to see the building taking everything on its chin like a seasoned street fighter, remain standing on its feet, and to shame the 'abusers' asks for knock out blows to be landed on it.

The only reference to its inception showing the linkage with the Miesian tradition is a beautifully designed glass box sitting at high level under the large roof to one side of the Market area, dissolving the space, looking down and reflecting the surrounding activities of this well crafted space.

The location of the large bulk of the building within the town is also brilliant.

It links various walking routes through and around it, addressing itself to a small town square, an open air market and car park and two main streets of the town.

Despite the size and bulk of the building, it sits majestically among the Victorian neighbours, with no visual niceties or concessions, without   playing second fiddle to anyone.

This building is a hidden gem (not visually exciting – more like an uncut precious stone) and has a lot of lessons to offer to many people of differing disciplines.

Down Radcliffe Street 40 years ago

Decay, Fire and Demolition

While Wolverton was in transition from a bust railway manufacturing town to a community where work was often to be found elsewhere, many of its industrial and public buildings fell into disuse. They thus became targets for vandals and arsonists.

Electrolux Fire

Electrolux Fire

Richie B. Is this the Electrolux fire? I was out getting lunch at the time saw a thin bit of smoke when I returned it looked like the end of the world at the bottom of Church St .. no one could get their cars out and I had to ferry people home

Jill G. I remember going into the co-op and coming out and there was this big black huge cloud of smoke and the smell my god, I lived in New Bradwell then and I could see it all from there I have some pics I took I will have to put them on.

Marc H. I was visiting Fred Adams in St Georges while this was going on and heard all the pumps turning up hell of a sight.

I had been out the brigade some years when this went up or properly would had been on the make up from Woburn Sands.

Nick Carter I was just going to start the late shift (2-10pm), when the fire broke out at a minute to two!...was a Friday, I recollect. I had to walk home to Linford, and came back on Monday morning. In the remains of my twisted locker was a melted safety helmet and a burnt jumper, but my chocolate bar was intact ! What does that say about Mars Bars ! lol

Terry L. No Marc I was on holiday again, in Spain I think, I missed quite a few of the big ones due to holidays :)

Phillip W. The smell from the fire was around for days.

Penny G. Does Electrolux still operate from there?

Phillip W. Yes they have had a new warehouse built

Jill G. My aunt's hubby works there.

Penny G. So the old train sheds were fortified for a new warehouse!?

Phillip W. Yes half of the old train shed collapsed in the fire

Penny G. Another bit of our heritage gone :((

Phillip W. Yes but they still one of the old sheds I was there before Xmas photographing it

Richie B. We were lucky we had the 2nd warehouse too continue trading and were lucky not to lose lives one girl only just managed to roll out under an automated fire door the alarm only rang once whilst we were in the building as the fire hit it so fast it only took 15 min before it was out of control take it from me that was the best of the two warehouse s

Richie B. It actually cost Electrolux 26 million in the end x

Offices Fire

Michael W. Me and Simon Moore remember it well...the first two to go in.

Phillip W. It looks bad I was told it was quite a bad fire. In the original plans for Tesco this building was supposed to be kept for housing.

Simon M. I never was so hot! It was the best fire I ever went too. Mick Wilson and me. Super crew!

Marc H . A nice shout for a Saturday evening I can remember make pumps what ever control unit canteen van we were on standby and then got mobilized from Bletchley

Simon M. I was at the fair Marc, saw the smoke and was first there. Bloody long time with just 3 of us until 2nd pump came. No saving that!!!!!

Terry L. I was thinking the other day the fair was on, but wasn't sure!

Marc H. Was this the one that the wall nearly came in on you and Mick!

Terry L. Yes a grueller that night Chief Fire Officer attended fire

Works Offices Fire

and had his wife with him; she wanted to go to the look so he brought her up to the Station and caught me and the Whitchurch boys with the bar open, and in full flow. Lol!

Marc H. Yes remember Mrs. Goddard sat in the car when Jeff rolled up.

Terry L. Is that Flash and Horse shit in the picture?

Marc H. Another good job was the Toby pub at Peartree Bridge another Saturday evening spent on the job LOL.

Terry L. Yep I caught that one, I was inside there with Jock Wylie and the Tiles were blowing off the roof!

Marc H. I remember the Whitchurch lads (323) call sign or was it Waddesdon (333)?

Simon M. The wall did come down Marc; I think it caught one of Towcester's boys? I just looked it is Horse Shit but don't if it's flash? Was with you at Peartree.

Simon M. That's Gt Holm's rescue pump at the front, so if that's our Water tender then it will be Flash.

Michael W. Remember it being dark and hot...we went in from the back by the Tesco road...and the other pumps couldn't find us...they didn't know the area like us.....quite scary with only 3 of us...seemed ages before we got any help.....the only water we had was in the pump...

Michael W. I do have some more will have to dig them out mate...

Terry L. Great Stuff Mick Didn't realise some of these existed!

John C. I remember my brother running round with firemen locating water hydrants for this fire, my brother worked for Anglia water.

Mike W. Remember the fire well; saw it from Top Rec, popped along to Stratford road to see the Wolverton crew turning out. Next hour or so the air was full of the sound of sirens. The heat from the fire was incredible; you could feel the heat from Church St.

Phillip W. It was a lovely building shame it went up

Marc H. Our system turn out take 144 to Bletchley for standby arrived in the pump bay got out 10 minutes later Bletchley turnout system went done and we joined you lot at Wolverton was a long night for all of us.

Science and Art Institute on Fire

Science and Art Fire

Elaine P. This photo shows The Science & Art Tech College on fire in the early 70s. This was taken from my bedroom window at no'32 Church Street....... this (& all the shops on that side) were all demolished to make room for the lovely Agora !!!!!!!! Behind this burning building is St.George's Church.

Jane B. I was there !!! Oh yes, it was a Thursday night (I'd just finished Brownies) in the summer - about 1970ish as I was 9 or thereabouts. We all sat on the Post Office windowsills and then our Dad's went over to Gregory's and got us all sausage and chips with scratchings !!! My God, that was a night and a half I can tell you.

Edith H. Yes I remember it well. Was just finished taking Rangers and we all rushed back to Guides to tell them. Nobody believed us.

Steve A. I was living in St Georges way at the time so was under 6 but still remember it well.

Constance O. I lived at 53 church St, and I remember them building that Agora. I remember that fire. My mum was crying.

Helen P. I remember you connie, I was Helen Lisle. I remember the science and art burning down too.

Julia B. I remember watching from somewhere along Church Street. Blimey.

Angie A. I was living in St Georges Way and I can remember the intense heat and the smells and sounds of that evening. I was Angela Willett then.

Sheila B. I think the whole of Wolverton where there

Linda K. Never saw this lovely building as it burned down a little while before I moved to the area.I would love to have seen it. Thanks for posting.

Pete B. I was on my way home from army cadets at the drill hall.

Terry L. I was there watching it with a bag of chips, watching the phone box melt. I heard rumors of who set it on fire and 2 names were mentioned ! I found out years later when I joined the local Brigade that as it was on a Thursday night, it was Drill night at Wolverton Station and 1 pump had gone out on training over Stony Stratford way, and the 2nd pump sat at the station. rather than call the 2nd pump they called the one from Stony and Newport Pagnell and the 2nd pump never even got tipped out to the fire, therefore it was S & A was lost !

Colin H. I remember my Eldest Brother, Frank, who was than a Volunteer Fireman, he nearly got flattened when the gable end collapsed and fell over ... He was placing a tray on the ground to collect the molten lead that was dripping off the roof ... Typical !!

Steph M. I remember reading about it in the Wolverton Express. The headline was "Science and Art - not Arson". I wondered who "Arson" was...............

Becca H. I remember the Science & Arts building fire really well. I stIll have an indented scar on my knee from that night. I was there with our mum and Christopher for certain but can't remember whether our sister and dad were there or not. Wherever we were walking or standing suddenly became more dangerous as bit of the building stated to cave in and collapse. We were told to run, and as I ran I tripped on a small iron stump sticking out of the ground and took a small chunk out my knee. I was later told by someone that there had been an iron fence or rail there previously that had been removed when the iron was needed for the war effort in WW2. We all talked about it for ages afterwards -

and it remains to this day one of the major historical events in our generation's Wolverton story.

Gill B. I remember when the Science & Arts building caught fire very well. I was in The Barrett at Northampton having just given birth to my son Gary. He was born on 23rd July 1970. My husband Geoff was late for visiting that evening as the fire had shut roads and he missed the train. Does not seem that long as my first year at the Grammar School was in that building.

Ian B. I could be in that photo. Was standing along there watching.

Marc H. we could see the smoke and flames from hanslope at the time wondered where it was coming from thought it was the works to start with

Helen P. Becca Hemmerman, are you Rebecca Gleadell? If so I remember you, and Lorna, and Chris. Also your mum and dad. I was Helen lisle, lived across the road.

Chris G. She is and I am too Helen, how you doing?

Ian S. i remember it all to well

Helen P. Hi Chris! Ent seen you for years! Last time was in the Bull in Stratford and I was with tracey Harding.

Chris G. Yeah I remember Helen, must have four or five years back at least? Hows life treating you?

Helen P. It was twelve years! I'm fine. Hope to see you all up the rec at the summer reunion!

Chris G. 12 years? Blimey don't time fly when you're enjoying yourself.

Helen P. Ha ha ha, yes!

Becca H. Helen Paton - Hello there! yes its me as my bro has already confirmed.

Tracy S. God Connie,I was at school with you. My name was **Tracy J.** Didn't you used to live near Irene Hepworth in Buckingham Street?

Kathleen A. I remember it well. We lived in St George's Way, the first one at the top of the steps. Hi Colin. How is Fank and where is he? When you see him tell him the Atkinson says hello that is paddy and co.

Keith B. I probably got blamed for it.

Terry L. Keith, think you were chasing Adders in the drill hall field that day !!

Elaine P. Here it is Sarah Louise Taylor !!!! xx

Steve P. Lived at the old chip shop, where the agora car park is now, at the time of this fire. Our potato shed & most of the neighbours sheds had an influx of rats soon after

Bryan D. Did they find out the cause of the fire?

Jane B. The rumour mill at the time Bryan said that a certain person (who shall remain nameless) was dared to light a fire in there - so they did and the result was as pictured above - don't think

Wolverton's Fire crew - Back Row: Simon Moore, Dean Williams, Terry Levitt, Andrew Dix, Steve Corcoran. Front: Geoff Twisleton/ Leading Fireman, Mark Harris/ Station Officer, Neil Stafford/ Leading Fireman

they thought for one minute it would go up like a tinderbox!!!! Still, gave us summat to do on a hot sultry Thursday evening (plus we got loads of chips from Gregorys Fish Bar - reckon he must have done a roaring trade that night) !!!!!!

Lynette M. Jane that is true I know who it was.

Bryan D. Hmmm! I'll have to wait for Inspector Clouseau to catch the Pink Panther.

Lynette M. Wolverton's best kept secret LOL

Carol R. I lived in a flat above Sketchley's cleaners next door to chippy at that time and remember it well.

Vivienne B. I Lived opposite, we all stood out side watching it burn lol

Marc H. We could see it from Hanslope but at first did not know what had gone up

Pete B. WHO DID DO IT ?

Anthony Z. I KNOW but will never tell

David E. Terry do you remember playing in there after school with Paul Lindop, Pete Gibbons, John Munday me and Les we used to climb through a window by the church. I didn't start the

Science and Art Institute after fire

fire tho, we could see it from Southern way it was well ablaze by the time we got down to church street

Paul L. I remember mucking abov inside.go caught by Rev Jones lol but i didn't set it ablaze.was there watching though !

Vivienne B. Hi Paul do you remember when your cousins came down from Liverpool, and we use to clown around in there? (hope you don't mind me saying Hi)

Paul L. Hi Vivienne I don't remember that .but their wasn't much else to do.back then lol

Pamela J. I used to go there for evening classes for extra Math and English.

Brian E. All that cheap tat on the stalls inside the Agora would make a lovely blaze!

Vivienne B. Hi Paul you may have been to young there names were Carol Sandra and Alan, Sandra Carol and I spent Hours over there lol

Vivienne B. Hi Mr Zastawny I remember you from our school days, I live round the corner from you and Janice (I think)

Tricia D. i think i / we ventured in there a couple of times - spooky!!

Julie W. If its the fire I'm thinking off he was seen running from the seen, we had some right scallywags in solve in the 60,s and 70's but we knew who they were and we're Part of us, so we never really bothered xx

Science and Art Institute Remembered

Andrew L. I never (that I can remember) got inside the Science and Arts building, and I always imagined it being lots of separate classrooms like a school. But this picture shows a big hall with study desks.

Science and Art Institute Hall.

Terry L. When I was a wee lad I found strewn across the back alley by the S&A caretakers house, some blue prints and diagrams and record books of the said S&A building. I believe we still have them tucked away somewhere!

Chris G. Were you with us when we went in that derelict house there Terry, seem to remember Glen Miller cutting his foot and needing stitches. There were old papers strewn everywhere, probably a goldmine to local historians today but I suppose they were buried in the rubble when it was demolished soon afterwards.

Terry L. Yes Chris, I think that's the time I picked them up or maybe I went back down there, but got a good thick carrier bag full of history !

Bryan D. They did have a hall upstairs Andrew. I remember it being used for photographic exhibitions and I think it was used for dances. There were classrooms and science labs as well, but I am sure that poster who actually went there will put us right.

Gill B. My first year at Grammar School was in the Science & Art building. I am sure it was small classrooms downstairs but upstairs was the hall with a stage. It also doubled up as a dining room

Science & Art Institute in its prime.

for school lunches and can remember hearing rats underneath the stage at meal times.

June L. They did use it as a Dance Hall, I took my friend Sheila who came to stay with me from London late 50s early 60s, Tommy Clarridge & his band use to play there, Eric Brae was his singer, there was also Doug Dytham, he used to play in the Works Hall.

Bryan D. Eric Bray. Great voice!

Andrew L. Presumably then, the picture above was taken from the stage. Are those windows in the picture on the Church St. side, or the St.Georges side?

Trevor I. Yes there was a dance hall in the S&A. My dad met my mom there during the war- asked her for a dance and the rest is history:).

Bryan D. Start of a good thread there Trevor. My parents too started going out together after a S & A dance. I bet that scenario was repeated thousands of times for that generation.

Trevor I. Yes I bet it was. Here's the full quick story. My dad bikes in from Wing air force base during war- to sat night dance at S&A. Sees my mom across the room- falls in love at first sight (he says). Goes up to her and says" I can't dance but I want to dance with you". They dance- get married and now I'm here:).

Andrew L. It's no wonder people were so sad when the place burned down then, must be a lot of sentiment and memories in there. I wonder how many people will be talking about how their parents met roller skating at the Agora.... :)

Trevor I. Who knows? - maybe there are some Agora love stories out there..

Linda K Andrew, plenty! I'm from Wolverton and adore all the old buildings. I wish they were more appreciated by the public in general. But my age means that for me it's the Agora that holds the most memories. Teenage years and all that! :-)

Chris G. Does anyone know what was planned for the S&A before the fire, it had stood derelict and unused for years, I guess demolition was on the cards anyway?

Linda K. I often imagine how grand and imposing it would look if it was still there. Better than the car park!

Chris G. And for years that car park was rough ground down rubble, making it even worse.

Jackie N. I bet it would be preserved now as part of the Conservation area. We used it (1958 and 1959) as we couldn't all fit into Moon Street.

Karen A. Such a shame it was knocked down, my Nan used to dance there every week, I bet lots of our grandparents did...

Science and Art: The Aftermath

Jackie N. Put this on, because I think it shows what a great building this was -all that architectural detail! I bet the shell would be saved now, even if the inside was remodelled and changed use -a badly missed opportunity there!

Colin T. The Crap Agora would never been built, You could of made the inside of this Beautiful Building into Shops, A meeting Place, some where nice to eat, An still have room for roller skating, xxxx......O Yeah & The people who live on the Square & beyond would still have direct access to there houses by car rather than going all round the back ways xxxx

Vivienne B. Spent many a happy hour playing in there, before the fire.

Linda K. Beautiful building. Great pic. Thanks for posting.

Margaret C. That's so much bigger than I remember, so good to see these photo's

Pete B. Why is there no proud buildings built any more?

Margaret C. Such a terrible waste...

Chris G. Should be remembered the place was standing derelict anyway and fire or not probably would have been gone sooner or later and all this pre any MK plans including the Agora. Jackie hit the nail on the head, now it would probably be saved, back then it was just another old small town white elephant building, unloved, unwanted and rapidly falling apart and like thousands of others around the country knocked down either for something new or because people couldn't afford its upkeep anymore. The Gleadells are originally a Gainsborough family and I've just joined their heritage group, in their picture archive they've got photo after photo after photo from the 50's, 60's & 70's of historic buildings just being eradicated either on some planners dream or mostly because they outlived their original usage. Having seen that whilst yep it would be great to have kept the S&A you realise how lucky Wolverton was in some respects and thankful for small mercies.

Terry L. Imagine what an indoor market that would of made !

Len E. The site is still a featureless car park

Matt R. What was the cause of the fire?

Colin T. Many--Many people have come up with diffrent things.....I think it was.......MATCHES lol xxxx

Chris G. No choice in the end Phil, so badly damaged through heat it was in danger of falling down.

David M. Thanks for a super picture. I would rather like to have a shot at making a model when I have time. Are there any drawings that anyone knows of that would have approximate dimensions?

Chris B. l Great picture. I have just found my dads school reports from there. Colin T , probably the funniest post ever!

Susan B. Such a lovely buiding, I wonder if it would still be there now if there was no fire

Jeffrey B. Oh boy did we get up to mischief at school..from 1958 until we moved to the new Radcliffe...(then it stopped)..what fun thanks for posting.

Paul S. Remember the night well. We were all coming out of a Thursday night band practice in the Works canteen. Awful!

Jackie N. Dad was always very keen on photography - he was a founder member of Wolverton Camera Club too. Not only that, he was very aware of the changes happening around us, as Milton Keynes developed and took it upon himself to record some of those changes, particularly in Wolverton - he had a great sense of history in the making.....

John C. Here is a wacky idea, why not rebuild it in the same place, same design and use it as a bus station and have the buses parking up next to it where carpark is now?

David M. Just for the hell of it I am tinkering around with photoshop to try and construct a card model of the old science and art. Sadly this picture is the best I have to work from which makes it tricky trying to warp the picture and change perspective to produce a flat front elevation. I don't suppose anyone has any pictures taken front on. I was poking around in the library to see if there are any architects drawings of the old place, but can't find any.

John C. How far up church street did this building go, it seems quite a long building?

John Sw. I know there have been photos like this posted before, but this looks even sadder transferred from a degraded slide. After the fire, June 1970. I agree that this was Wolverton's best building.

Steve A. The old place did have some pretty impressive buildings didn't it?

Margaret Ck. The building just in the picture on the right was the Sketchley Dry Cleaners......we lived in the flat there for a while.

Chris G. After the S&A had gone we used to play in the deserted house on the left, it was full of old documents, all probably lost now sadly but would have been a treasure trove for the likes of Bryan & Phil.

Terry L. No, I rescued the documents, and they are now in a cellar in Wolverton.

Chris G. I remember a mutual friend of ours getting quite a stamp collection off those old papers from that house Terry.

Terry L. There were a load strewn around the house and alley, and I picked handfuls up, don't know what condition they are in now, but I will find out.

Pam F. Apparently my uncle Harry Lawless had some of his paintings there. He was quite an artist. If you find any ....

Terry L. Says who ?

Terry L. I am very happy for them to go to the museum, I will ask the man that is the keeper of the documents, if it is viable!

Cricket Pavilion

Harvey A. I don't think I've seen this picture of the old cricket club pavilion on here before. About the winter of 1957/8 dad and one or two others set about re-vamping the place. The veranda was enclosed and a multi-coloured decoration scheme was implemented

Karen L. Ohhhh, the mystery!!! lol x

Harvey A. Lawrie played in the last season I was at Wolverton (1959), but our lives didn't cross very much. The others were after my time, I guess.

Karen L. To the best of my knowledge, many players that have been mentioned started in the 50's (or before) and went on to the 70's (and after)??? Such is cricket!!

Mike L. Harvey, Pete Lloyd was my father (sadly no longer with us). Thanks for the story (can understand why you removed it - not exactly PC). Would love to share any others you have. A couple of David Lloyd's children (Geoff & Maryanne) are also members on here. I'm busy looking back through old posts - I posted a couple of pictures from just before and just after you played for Wolverton. If I find them I'll bring them back to the top of the

The Old Cricket Pavilion

board for you (if not I can always post them again.
Mike L. Pam, I played with Bob, Lol and Trevor.
Harvey A. Thanks Mike. Yes, having put it on I felt uncomfortable about it, so removed it. Thanks also for correcting your relationship. I owe a great debt to the senior members of that team, your dad included. They gave me and other youngsters a lot of encouragement and opportunity. There was a community spirit about the side that was part of the 'Wolverton feeling' of that time and that others have mentioned over the last few months.

The Pineapple
John S. Who remembers the Pineapple club?
Ian S. Had a game of tennis there Saturday morning
Kevin S. Played cricket and hockey there
Sheila B. Have lived opposite for 34 years
Chris G. I bet you miss seeing that every morning Sheila, must break your heart.
Hazel S. It is now Pineapple segments at Stembridge in Somerset.
Pat B. I used to clean for a while at the Pineapple. It was a devil of a place with coarse matting and a hoover that would not pick up. Not to mention the huge overhead yellow trunking that went round the upper floor of the building.... Strange building!!!
Jackie S. Lol, Hazel.
Terry L. I was in the Sports club (not Shop) last week and Marion told me that the building is still the same as then but without the

The "Pineapple" under construction

shell on it, and they still have an upstairs which is not used now but could be converted into a nice space!

Hazel S. To view the Pineapple in its final days as a structure you need to go to Google Earth and put in the following coordinates 50.976492N 2.833375W (Maximum Zoom). Initially you won't recognise what is on view, but move the timeline slider back to any date before the year 2006 and there you have it. Burrow Hill Cider Farm have developed this site and as you would expect in Somerset apples have become more popular than pineapples!!

Kevin S. Great find Hazel.......and somewhere to pass by when next in Somerset!!

Terry L. Thanks Hazel , I will post the picture up top..

Stephen Godfrey I remember it well, spent many hours in there.

Rita B. Yes I used to live in Victoria St. Didn't go there only for jumble sales; helped out on a stall.

Len E. My only recollection of the Pineapple is smashing my watch at a News Years eve disco. My own fault - being pissed and trying to dance was not a good combination.

Susan B. Remember it well, spent a few months in there with my ex boyfriend

Rita B. Susan got a feeling I know you from school what was you maiden name

Vivienne B. OMG That's a think from the past.

Wolverton Park

Bryan D. Here is a photo taken in the Park in 1967 or 1968. They appear to be playing without nets.
Martin G. Happy memories.
Ian H. You can just make out how they had to encroach on the track to allow for the corner!!
Jane N. My dad, Rodney Cleaver used to play football here, he was a goalie.
Paul S. Remember your dad Jane. Great servant to WTFC.

Football at Wolverton Park

Terry L. A very unique pitch for corner kicks Ian Hickson.
Martin G. Remember playing there for Bucks Schools,many years ago.
Ian H. Terry Boz you wait 'til you go to the "Golden Palace" mate
Chris B. Nets are up in my high definition computer Bryan!
Michael M. Aagh! sports day, egg and spoon etc.
Bryan D. Ive just looked at the original Chris. I can see them at the sides, although not very visible at the back. No unnecessary chasing after the ball in that case.
David Old this looks like wolverton minors they were reformed in 1967-8 I have a photo of the team somewhere.
David J. Bagged a few at that place
Chris G. And reformed again mid to late 70's under the management of Clive Meakins. I scored twice in the trial game, both in that end. Never scored again all season, doh!
Ian Hs. Proper game linesmen. Number 2 in goal squad numbers?

Pat B. Donna, this made your Father in law laugh out loud

Ken C. I played for Wolverton minors in about 1968-1970. We came 2nd in the north bucks league in 69-70 I think. Then there was a match between us and 1st place Northampton team at the top rec. at the end of the season.

Ken C. I could name most of the team then. Robert Lindop in goal, (and later Roger Knight). Ian Ferguson(Danny's younger brother) and myself full-backs. Paul Kightley, Paul Dewick and Ian Drury half-backs. Keith Eales, Michael Millard, Phil Church (I think) in the forwards.

Ken C. Bryan, was it taken on a Sunday afternoon?

Bryan D. Sorry Ken, I have no precise date. I don't even know why I was there or why I took the photo. It was just a single frame.

Adrian C. Fond memories of the Park. The Craufurd pub team played there for a couple of seasons where flattened out the corners. I think we got chucked out for drinking too much beer. Was it Tuborg Gold on tap ?

Football spectators from the 1950s

Chris G. We were stitched up Tich, did loads of work there (including those corners), put loads more behind that bar than the senior club (Wolverton Town), organised various do's there etc, but jealousy by some at WTFC who couldn't see their nose for their face caused an argument where they accused of of trying to take over The Park when in all truth at that time it was our money keeping the place afloat and all we wanted was a place to play not take over. The main instigator behind it is dead now I believe so I won't name him here but we all know what happened a season or so later. What they could have done with our cash then eh?

Adrian C. Remember winning that championship, beating Bletchley Arms 1-0 great times

Paul S. What happened at the park was little short of criminal Chris. Bad management and greed prevailed, never mind about our clubs history!

Chris G. Indeed Paul and all pushed to oblivion by an outsider when all is said and done, promised the earth and delivered nothing.

Sarah T. My dad had a lot to do with Wolverton football club, we use to go there a lot.

McCorquodales

The history of McCorquodales in Wolverton is almost as long as the railway. They were invited to establish a factory in Wolverton to provide employment for young women in the period between leaving school and marriage. They were already established as the printer of choice for the L&NWR and in 1878 they built an envelope factory at the western edge of town. The plant started with 120 women and grew to over 1,000. They were printers for large scale industries like the L&NWR and also took on government contracts, and during that period were subject to high level security.

McCorquodale's Printing Works

Ruth E. Did anyone work at McCorquodales?

Stan Butler I did! Worked there for 45 years as a compositor McCorquodale's was a family run firm. One of the family, Hugh, was at one time married to novelist Barbara Cartland. A number of my family worked there. First there was my Mother who was there prior to 1939 and by the time that I started work in 1954 I was joining 4 uncles and 2 aunts. We were later joined by another uncle 2 cousins and my sister. (Hope I haven't left anyone out.) All worked in various departments including the Post office Security dept. The working week was then 42 1/2 hours and an apprenticeship was 6 years. Mine was halted after 5 years when I did my stint of National Service at 21. Which was about to come to an end. About 500 men an women were employed at this time working alongside each other, and at times this did cause some domestic problems, although many a girl from the print married a chap from the works.

On the north side or the road were the Offices, Binders Dept, Rulers Dept. Envelope Room, Rotary, Print Room and the case room for Compositing. Certain Security work called for some of us to have to sign the Official Secrets Act.

On the south side of the road was the Canteen/Reading Room. Post Office Printing Dept and Electrical Engineers Department. Small Fork lift trucks were often seen nipping across the road to unload huge paper rolls from delivery lorries. Delivery of more modern printing machinery would cause a stir, like when colour printing became the new thing. During the daytime the Canteen served hot meals to employees and was used as a library to while away lunchtime. At night it was used for social events, Film shows, dancing and parties. It had facilities for Snooker, Darts and Table Tennis. It had it's own Football Team and a Social Club Committee headed by Reg Russell from Anson Road, Well known for his organization skills. The occasional coach trip was arranged and a float was usually entered in the Carnival Parade.

The Printing trade moved on from Lead letter press printing to Lithographic to Photographic printing and with modernization the number of employees was much less and the whole of the business was transferred to the south side of the road around late 1980's (Not sure about date) There had been two new owners. Norton Opax and the Rexam. The old Buildings were demolished. I am sure there is lots that I have left out and If I think of anything else I will let you know. I hope that some of the younger employees will remember one or two funny stories. All I know is that their Pension Scheme keeps me going today and the gold watch they gave me keeps perfect time.

Ian H. Did you get a watch or some Postal Orders when you retired Stan?

Mr. GEORGE McCORQUODALE
(Founder of the Company)

McCorquodale & Co. Ltd.

Centenary Celebrations

Saturday, October 5th, 1946

Wolverton

McCorquodale Centenary. Brochure

Theresa W. Hi Stan, I used to work at MCP in office with Mick Little, Keith Day and Steve Moore, was Bailey back then x
C. Ross Hi Stan Butler. I worked in the offices from 1967 to 1972 and was a Work Study Evaluating Clerk and calculated the Compositors weekly bonuses.
Ron B. My wife Margaret Baker worked for Ted Pankhurst in personnel

Andrew L. My mum (envelopes) and grandmother worked there, covering 1950s right up until the last days of MCP and Bong.

Celia R. I worked in the envelope room in 1962 for a while before I got married

Richie B. Dad worked there for years was something to do with the union at one point drove a lorry for a while I remember going out in that and he worked in the newer warehouse Church St end packaging I think ..

Ian H. My sister Mary Cox worked there for years, on the PO side.

Diane K. Did you see the pic I posted of the mccorqudales dance both my Nan Lillian Levie and dads wife Marjorie Crossan (was Lowry) worked there

Emma P. I worked in the envelope room as a temp in 93.

Tracy S. My husband's granddad worked in the print for years - Jack Batterick. Don't know if anyone would remember him.

Julie K. I worked in the print machine dept. for 8 years, 79ish to 86ish. Will have to try and remember some suitable stories, the one's I can remember are not printable. My maiden name was Robinson, my brother Steve worked in the warehouse for a few yrs., our step dad George Green was manager of Print Dept. until I started there then he became sick, not my fault I might add, it turned out he had cancer and died a year later in April 1980, and I must agree Clarence Gill is a lovely man, he was very supportive to my family as was Charlie Broadhust. It has been many years since I have seen or thought of these guys, so thanks for jogging my memory.

Ruth E. Ah come on Julie bet you can clean a story or two up xxx

Julie K. Can't remember his name but when I first started to work there he got a little too close for comfort, sometime later myself and another girl locked him in the trim room, and wouldn't let him out until he had stripped down to his boxers, we hid his cloths, his face was a picture and I am sure he lean't his lesson, he had the reddest face ever, and he never reported us, I wonder why!

I used to do the late shift 1pm to 8pm I think it was, one of us used to go and get fish and chips, I remember going back hyper and tormenting our printer, won't say who he is, he picked me up and put me in a paper skip (deep sided) could not get out, spent what seemed like half an hour laughing my socks off, eventually my work mate June got a chair for me to climb out onto. Didn't stop us teasing him though. He was also terrified of spiders, a huge one crawled out of a box I picked up, I dropped it silent screamed and froze pointing at it and he ran a mile, didn't see him for an hour, my work mate at that time I think was Joyce Levitt she sorted out the spider, then me.

Another thing I remember is the sound of the crickets in there, early in the morning, before any machines were turned on. God knows what it was like at night, cricket and spider parties.

June L. I been trying to think back to when I worked there Ruth, I started there in 1957 first in the Binding room on a pager then on a Numerator machine, Forman was named Charlie? Then a fore lady Margaret, she made news in the Wolverton Express for long service to Macs. I worked with Sylvia Bull (not June as I said before) Sylvia introduced me to Pete my husband 1957 in the Plough pub. I also worked in there with Anne & Betty Henderson who lived in Oxford St @ the time, Betty married Donald Scott from Green Lane.

Julie K. Worked with Don Scott...

Stan B. To, Tracy S. . I remember Jack Batterick very well and to June Levitt, was the foreman you were thinking of, Charlie Walding?

Tracy S. Thanks for that Stan, nice to think that someone remembers him.

Lee F. My granny (Nancy Richardson) worked there all her working life, not sure which department she was in though.

Helen P. Knew your Nan Lee, and Fred, also Colin and Debbie.

June L. I didn't know Charlie's surname so you may be right Stan.

Ruth E. Thank you all bit of info there see Julie K. I knew you would find a little gem somewhere. Massive thanks to Stan who e mailed me some info.

Jackie N. I think this was just before demolition (dated 1988)

Barry L. I see it still has the green doors leading into the envelope

McCorquodale's in 1910

room did they ever paint them? they were just the same when I worked there in the early 70's.

Tracey W. Haven't seen any of this since the 70s. Has all the big wall gone, and what is there now? You would have thought they would have made it into a big shopping complex.

Chris G. Robert B. did I imagine this or did you have an orange Beetle around this time? I know Steve Hayfield had a couple too, not this colour though.

Sharon A. Just got married that year, just passed my driving test x x

Robert B. Chris we did have a bright orange mini around that time. It had the trendy "Jeans" interior.

Phillip G. My late father worked in the large machine room his name was Stan Gammage worked on the Heidelberg.

Hilary R. I worked in the binding department and my mother worked in the envelope room her name is Alma Eaton hello Philip remember me ?

Phillip G. Yes I do you used to live at 9,Green Lane next to the Ridgeway's where are you know I am at the bottom of Green Lane it's called Bushfields

Hilary R. I live in Kingsthorpe Northampton been here 39 year dont come back to Wolverton much now its not the same dont seem to know many people in wolverton now. how are you are you married

Phillip G. No I am single and I care for a lady in New Bradwell and take her shopping. Hospitals and Doctors also take her dog out clean and cut her grass we go to St George's Church for soup Fri Breakfast Sat and Sun in my leisure time I play Cricket for wolverton and go to The County Ground Northampton to watch Northants at Cricket.

Barry L. pity there's not more caring people like you out there Philip .

Hilary R. He was always a caring person.

Peter A. Aaaah! so that's what my mum meant when she said to me as a kid that theres a bug going round Wolverton.

Mark B. Spent many hours looking through the vents to see what was going on inside, or watching the lorries unload huge rolls of paper when I was little and we were walking up to Wolverton from the Galleon estate.

Toni B. Awww...happy days. ..

Michael W. a sad day...another piece of history gone..

Richie B. Used to wait outside them huge doors waiting for my sister to finish work many years ago.

Andy Ck. Used to go to the kids Xmas party when my Dad worked there.......sad it's gone.

Doreen B. wished it was still all there, happy times we had...xxx

McCorquodale's Envelope Room

Steph M. My dad used to buy his paper there from offcuts. He'd go into the office where everyone always seemed to be drinking strong tea - early 1960s. There was a floor worker who would take him to the paper stoors. He was a little man - probably middle aged and always seemed to be carrying an enamel jug full of paraffin - funny how these things stick in your memory after all these years. My dad passed away in 1989 but I still have some old McCorq's offcuts of paper that he never used!

Debbie S. Worked there for many years,with my mum and dad.... good times..

Celia R. I worked there 1962 in envelope room

Debbie S. My mum and dad were Walter & Val Kay Did you know them...

Celia R. The name rings a bell but can't remember off hand.

Peter L. I know Walt well, often talk to him up the club, nether of us are in the best of health so we have a lot to talk about.

Debbie S. Ohh wow you know my Dad hes a moany old bugger.... lol...He lives in the club...bless him..

Doreen B. Which club does your dad go in? Top or Bottom? lol,xxxxxx

Julie K. Hi Debbie. Bit late on here, but I worked with your dad in the Rotary machine print room and your Mum in the Finishing Dept. You worked in there too didn't you? and Doreen Beckwith?

Richie B. My Dad and Sis both worked there at some point.

Debbie S. My Dad goes to the top and bottom club...and I worked there for about 20 years or so....now live in Michigan in the USA.

Part Two:

Room for Reminiscence

Part Two
ROOM FOR
REMINISCENCE

Air Travel

Ian H. Remember your first flight!! Mine was from Manchester to Glasgow in 1970 for work purposes, didn't like to tell the MD I hadn't flown before, phew!! It was for Rocla Pipes.

Jennifer T. Mine was about 1973, from Luton to Mallorca, with Maura Nina pat and 5 other friends from the top club (ladies only)

Ian B. First was 1970, BOAC 707 London to Beirut second was MEA Caravelle Beirut to Amman. Would have been OK but earlier the PLF had hijacked and blown up 3 aircraft at Dawson's field in Jordan.

Bryan D. 1968 London to Amsterdam. Phew!!

Chris G. Dan Air Comet to Venice in 1978 to start school cruise. And the novelty of having two lines of seats facing each other with a table in the middle.

Brian E. Not a flight exactly. But the Hover speed Hovercraft from Dover to Calais. It sort of flies! This was 1971.

Jackie S. 1976 to Sweden aged 16.

Becca H. Ear Drum Busting 88 seater DC-4 1976 to Douglas, Isle of Man

Constance O. Mine was in 1980, moving to the USA

Brian E. I have often flown from Mexico City to Guadalajara on Aero México Douglas DC10s. Very old jets. Because Mexico City is half way up a mountain, and Gaud. Is low lying, the aircraft does not ever seem to climb. So, all the way, you can see the ground clearly. Roads, cars, even people. Being accustomed to being miles up, this is a spooky experience. The pilots' cock-pits are all leather and dials, a bit like a WW2 bomber.

Jane B. When I was 14 months old flying from Glasgow to South Uist - not that I remember it clearly. The second time was in 1985 when I flew to Paris - and haven't stepped on a plane since - I was absolutely bloody terrified - so no more air travel for me thank you very much!!!!

Donna S. May 21st 1976... London to Toronto Canada. Age 12

John R. I don't remember the plane, but it was in jump school while I was in the army. Interesting experience, my first flight and then being told to jump out of the side door.

Susan H. Mine was in 1971 age 17 - Luton to Barcelona with Court Airlines, courtesy of Clarkson Holidays! £34 for 10 days bed, breakfast and evening meal. My first holiday without the old folks.

Ruth E. 1968 to Malta with Chris and his Mum she has not been back since the war. Chris asked if I wanted an engagement ring or a holiday I plumped for the hols, but still got the ring later.

Ian H. You know Ruth Berry I so remember your mum in law, especially her hair which was the complete opposite colour of her hubby, very pretty lady. Did she fly to England as a bride or by ship from Malta?

Ruth E. I believe by ship she married in Malta war bride. very pretty lady she is 86 now I still see her now and then .I think I have put a pic on this site somewhere only a small one in her wedding dress.

Ian B. John R. never saw the point in jumping out of a perfectly good plane.

Julia B. Some UK airport to Alicante Spain, en-route to Benidorm!!! With Sue Finch from Stony, I was 18 and fell for a Spanish waiter name of Jesus, even went to meet his mum! more funny memories!

Becca H. I did a couple of parachute jumps for "Save the Children" charity in the late 80's - and it was fab! Also love abseiling and done loads of that for both pleasure and for various charities over the years.

Becca H. Oh no Julia - did you meet him too!!!

Julia B. Yes Becca and he told me he wanted me for a sunbeam! :))))

Becca H. ....yeah - it was when he told me he wanted you, me, two lasses from Coventry, one from Doncaster and another from Droitwich for his heavenly solar selection I thought it sounded dodgy Julia - so I grabbed his.... complimentary jug of sangria and flip flopped it off to Torremolinos! x

John R. Ian: It wasn't really a voluntary exit - there was a great deal of motivation from from a very large, and from what I remember, unpleasant instructor.

Jackie S. Becca and Julia, how I wish I had known you two at school.

Becca H. As opposed to the teachers of mine and Julia's class Jackie, who wished they WEREN'T at school with us 2! Xx

June L. I think it was America, Chicargo. Pete & I went there for our Silver Wedding Anniversary & stayed with Pete's sister & Horst our brother-in-law

June L. Becca. You are brave to parachute, I'm terrified of heights, I'm ok in a jumbo but when we were in Austria & I had to go up the mountains in a chair lift by myself my legs really turned to jelly, worst coming down the mountain because you are looking into space & swaying in mid-air.

Becca H. Thanks June x I just loved that kind of thing. I did one off the top of the huge Citibank building in Lewisham once with the Royal Marines. They were fab trainers and I got picked to do more training with them - being the dummy accident casualty up a mountain. Loved it. However, have never liked those ski lift type chairs as I had an irrational fear of my boots falling off and crashing to the ground (even though they were tied on with 'industrial strength laces four times) x

Terry L. Me too, First plane I went in was a Cessna at Bridlington for a charity parachute jump!

Becca H. Me too Terry Boz - that's where I did mine!! xx

Jill G. Mine was Romania 1974

Terry L. Wow, snap Becca , did you land in a field which was being combined at the time as well?

Becca H. OMG - yes! In fact there was a big fuss that I was completely unaware of because my parachute 'ribboned' and didn't open as quickly as it should. I was completely unaware of it as I was still busy chanting the counting thing to myself. Anyway, they sent the med team rushing out to me when I landed as they thought I would be in shock etc. I was lying on the ground, laughing my head off and adrenaline up to the eyeballs - and just thought they were doing a dummy practice run. Went along with the "story" as the dummy victim - and egged it up a bit - till I saw my (then) husband appear in another truck, rushed out - with tears in his eyes. WTF I thought, I am a good actress but he is doing better than me. I only realised when someone played a little cam film thing to me what had happened. I was fine and loved it - and would go up again that day - but no one else there with me could stand it. Xx

Terry L. I was nervous and they had to push me out, but soon as I was down I wanted to go up again but it was too late in the day :-(- never done it again since.

John R. My first landing was really uneventful, just sort of drifted down and everything worked as planned. Aside from the normal nerves, who in their right mind jumps out of a perfectly serviceable airplane, I was also concerned that the parachute

He was packed correctly, seeing as I had to do that as well! No, the first jump was fine, it was the last one that did my in, hit the roof of a building, got all tangled up, and broke my leg.

Allotments

Bryan D. After Julia mentioned the newt pond earlier I went into my photo archive to find this. I took this in the mid 1960s up in the allotments past Furze Way, so I think this may be the pond that Julia was talking about. I have no idea why I took this picture, probably because of the junk in the pond.

Wendy C. If you knew where the playgroup was it was next to that....its still there but is more of a hole now :-(

Becca H. Did we at one time call this Barley's pond or was that a different pond?

John R. I think that's it.

Becca H. Yes the description of the location is right. Spooky pic

Newt Pond at the old allotments

for me cos we kept our newts we got from there (in jam jars) in a tin baby bath in the garden.

Jane B. I fell in there when I was 9 - jeez, I nearly wet myself as the pond contained frogs and I have a phobia about them !!!! Ran home crying with wet socks and plimsolls - got told off as "I should have watched what I was doing" - the joys of childhood eh?

Kim P. Bill Elliott's railway carriage on the allotments today. I don't recall its early history other than that it was built at the Works (in the late 1800's I believe) but it ended up in Anson Road in the garden of Bill Elliot's house, where he used it as an office for the Works Union. If anyone has the book "Piano and Herrings" about Bill's life, it is in there.

Jane B. It arrived one lunchtime through the Marron Lane gate accompanied by Tony Marshall, Lynne Marshall and 4 or 5 others. Was pushed on rollers down the narrow riding towards Tony's allotment but for some reason stopped half way and sat there for a day or two until it was finally moved into it's position on the allotment. Looked somewhat incongruous stuck on the ridings I can tell you - and think Tony was more than a touch embarrassed about the predicament !!! Still, all's well that ends well as you can see by the photo !!!!!

Bryan D. What a great story!

Kim P. I think it's interesting to follow the carriage's path through

the decades. If you have access to the Piano and Herrings book, there is a photo of Bill on the back cover in the carriage from the time he used it as the union office.
Chris G. Great story Kim.

An adapted railway carriage - once common in Wolverton

Behind the Walls

Andrew L. Somebody will know what went on behind these walls.In my imagination there were thousands of oompa-loompas pouring molten chocolate into railway train shaped moulds while singing:

> Oompa-loompa dompadee doo
> We've got another carriage for you.

John Rd. Well behind that wall is a load of very expensive houses now. Too expensive for Wolverton that's for sure
Andrew L. Unless you find a golden ticket.
Chris G. And 'Pigeon Poo' Bridge in the distance...
Faye L. Always wondered what it looks like on the other side of that wall xx
Phillip W. I have photos of the inside of that wall when it was workshops
Faye L. No I meant how it looks now; x
Phillip W. Loll I have photos of that too
Faye L. Oh well put one up man loll xx
John Rd. They are not bad but for around 250k for a 2bedroom timber frame house isn't that great. Wolverton Park isn't cheap. A 1 bedroom flat is around 160k in the new builds....much rather buy a place on Buckingham street. 3 bed for around 120-130k :)

Works buildings backing onto Canal

Chris G. You can walk through there Faye.

Faye L. I knew that of course lol.

John Rd. Just go to the Knight Frank office in the triangle building with your fella a say you're looking at buying one and ask to look at the show home. But whatever you do....don't buy one for God sake!!

Faye L. As I want one of them loll plus we can't afford it xx

John Rd. Even if I was a multi billionaire I still would not buy one.

Julie K. What I fail to understand is what kind of people would buy and actually want to live there!

Andrew L. Oompa-Loompas would live there!

Julie K, Ha loll... would love to see that!

John Rd. Not many to be honest. When I left my job there last September only 1 or 2 houses in that building out of 20 were sold. A few were being rented out. There is also 26 flats/maisonettes in there too which were selling/renting but they are also timber framed so you can hear your neighbours washing machine upstairs shaking the floors. plus never....I repeat never buy brand new timber frame homes.... always wait till they are at least 5yr's old so you know they have settle otherwise you're going to be filling a lot of cracks for a while. Also the main problem with the timber frames on this site is they don't support the roof. So they are constantly shrinking and expanding with the seasons.

Julie K. Well there you have it, we will leave it for the Oompa-

Loompas then, joking aside I much prefer to live in a solid brick built house with a view and not a brick wall, worked in Mac's for 8 yrs. so have seen enough walls to last me a life time.

John Rd. Timber frame is ok if you live in a bungalow...cheap to build with but as soon as you want that 1st floor or more than traditional build is the only way to go to be honest

Julie K. I agree with you, come from a family of builders, watched some been built near where I live, all timber frame bought in and put together in no time would not want to live in one.

Bryan D. I grew up in a brick house with the belief that brick was superior to timber, yet after I moved to North America where most houses are timber built I started to reconsider that view. Apart from the fire risk, timber houses last longer. Brick buildings seem to have a shorter life span. Take a look around Wolverton and Stony Stratford and. You will find that the older buildings by far are the wooden ones.

Pat C. From personal experience, heating leaks can be bad enough if not found in block/brick but can be really messy in timber frame!

John Rd. Timber frame is good in places where you don't get a lot of rain but in England they are not much use at all with our piss poor weather. also I can't think of any timber frame buildings in Wolverton that are old and I certainly don't buy that brick house don't last considering the amount in the up that are hundreds of years old going back to the 16th century when they were became more common built (I won't make a case for stone buildings which have been standing for even longer)

Phillip W. Here's a question to all those living in Wolverton in 60's and 70's ,what was it like living in Wolverton with steam and diesel trains and shunter engines . and was it noisy with the works?

Andrew L. Traverse sirens, works whistle, Fire siren and trains rattling round Moon's curve are the sound of my youth.

Phillip W. I really wish I had the chance to spend a few weeks in Wolverton in the days of steam but that will never happen

Bryan D. No sound came from behind the wall and once the men had gone inside at 7:43 the doors closed - and silence. Most of the day was punctuated by the rush of passing trains - the noise rose to a crescendo and the, true to the Doppler Effect, immediately fell away. It was a sound we all got used to and largely ignored. There was no road traffic noise and very few cars in the 1950s. In the whole of Windsor St there were four car owners, for example. It was avert quiet place - like a remote country village today.

Phillip W. Does anyone know when the works steam shunters were changed?

Richie B. You can occasionally hear the high speed trains pass through still but I miss the siren :)

Lesley W. The Works siren. That brings back memories.

Sheila H. The works siren, the rag and bone man, Vic the milkman, The man from the Pru, hearing the trains at night when tucked up in bed under Mum's coats, playing in the street and kicking the leaves in autumn down Marina Drive ..... and many more memories! Wish I could go back for a day :(

Ian H. Me too Sheila but as a child.

Sheila H. That's what I meant - as a child

Ian H. This site is a very good alternative though' and get's better and better.

June L. Terry was a engine driver, can't remember if it was diesel but he always pressed the Hooter (if it was called that) as he came pelting though Wolverton station so I knew it was him late evenings.

Steve A. Living in St George's way in the 60s there used to be a fair bit of noise from Dunlop and Rankin especially at night, in the summer I used to lie in bed and listen to it, it was quite comforting, you'd hear the 'tea up' shout at about 9.pm

Phillip W. I live in St. Georges' Way at the moment there is a fair bit of noise that comes from Electrolux and the works shunter when it bring stock in and takes stock out

Brian E. I can remember Bacals building the electrification pylons. Back then, steam was being phased out. To me, then, steam was old hat, and diesels were a novelty. So I used to hope we got a new diesel when we went on holiday or trips, although it was usually a steamer.

Chris G. Heard a travvy siren the other day walking past the works, not heard one in years.

Phillip W. What was it like living near the works goods yard with the shunters going around

Kathy P. Used to now we were late back to school in afternoon if we heard the " works " hooter going and run like hell to get . and Wolverton was like a ghost town in the 2 week summer shut down , happy days .

Jackie N. One of my earliest memories is lying in bed and listening to the trains (this would be 1950s, so still steam) - and we lived in Oxford Street! - mind you the wind had to be in a certain direction.........

Carnival

Susan H. A photo of the Works Carnival entry for 1971, there's me and Lynn Crossman - any other help in naming names would be appreciated. — in Wolverton.

Ian H. If you read the print Susie they are named, it's not too clear but is readable.

Ruth E. Michael Chaytor in the middle I was at school with him. And Lyn Crossman married my cousin Colin Read. Divorced now.

Ian H. Technocrat!!

Susan H. Ahhhh, wish I had thought of that! In the middle of having a new kitchen built so my poor aged little brain is too confused x

Davd O. Brian Scripps sitting on the right.

Kevin S. Mick lives in the US now.........if I'm not mistaken

The Works Apprentices' entry in Wolverton Carnival 1971, (winners) depicting *The Railway Children*, from the film. L to R standing: D. Payne, P. Hill, F. Andrews, A. Neal, R. Thorn, Miss L. Crossman, Miss S. Curtis; L to R sitting: G. Digby, M. Chaytor, B. Scripps.

BR Carnival Float

Carpentry Skills

Phillip W. Did you know the works didn't just make carriages and wagons? They also made desks, chairs, cupboards, notice boards and station seats and other things for stations

Bryan D. That's an interesting fact Phillip. I wonder if there are still some carpenters or cabinet makers out there who remember doing such work.

Phillip W. There may well be

Ron B. They made all the pews in St George's church as well. The wood block floor came out of the works

Bryan D. Curiouser and curiouser. What about the wood block flooring in the Church Institute, and the school - Church St., Aylesbury St., Moon St.?

Chris G. Talking of block flooring there were sections of wooden floor in The works in the old grinding shop and 'caves' under Stratford Road made up of old Victorian wooden wheel segments

LNWR Exhibition Stand made in Wolverton

off the trains, all cleverly done and fitted together, apparently it was all very hard wearing teak. Was there when I left early 80's so guess still there when it was all knocked down.

Ron B. Probably came from the works as well Bryan. When I painted the inside of St Georges quite a few years ago, the cross beams hadn't been cleaned for ages. After cleaning we found the name of the painters who did it in 1937.

Bryan D. I don't know about the other places but the Church Institute (Madcap) still has its original block flooring - a little loose in places but still there after 104 years.

Brian E. I wonder if Moon Street School still has its blocked flooring.

Wendy C. Last time I was in there it was still there....

Bryan D. Well, there you go! The Pineapple comes and goes; the Agora comes and is going . . . . . but the wood block flooring, trodden by hundreds of thousands of feet, goes on forever.

Brian E. Agora, built in last 30 years - floor coming up, peeling & uneven. Market, school, built over 100 years ago; floors still perfect! Ummm...

Bryan D. It illustrates a problem for our times. Years ago things were built to last and even to be handed down through the generations but now we chuck things out long before they wear out. I was told earlier this year that Sony (who once had a reputation for quality) use the same crappy components as everyone else but charge for the label. They have figured out that the average consumer will move on to the latest version before their old one begins to wear down. Can it go on like this?

Phillip W. A lot of the old office furniture from the old office was made at Qolverton it was a very self-contained work place. It made everything.

Brian E. I think it was Ford who introduced built-in obsolescence in their cars in the seventies. Instead of "built to last" their new slogan was altered in a horribly Orwellian way. It became, "built to last 3 years." We see this now with insurance deals on nearly every electrical item we buy from the likes of Curry's. And, in MK, compare the facades of the Victorian.

Pauline D. My husband made Level crossing gates, signal boxes, and furniture for railway stations, he was in the works from 1957 - 1964- ~ Robert Devereux.

Lee P. My great grandparents had a long wooden bench in the back garden of their house in Stacey Avenue that had the raised letters "Wolverton" on the back rest. I assume it came from the station. It was pretty decrepit when I used to work in the garden back in the late 70s and disappeared soon after. If only....

Phillip W. It may have ended up at the museum as there is one just like it up there.

Lee P. Maybe, although my Nan was pretty rigorous when it came to tidying up the garden and my Gramp's stuff after he died. While you're here, have you ever looked at the Works employee record cards that I remember once having a rummage through at Stacey Hill? I found out from my Gramp's record that he was sacked from the Works for being asleep on the job.

Phillip W. I am on the surname being with c at the moment I find so interesting but also hard as I have not been taught how to read old fashioned writing.

Brian E. Is it in Copperplate writing, Philip? That was generally how clerks were expected to write.

Phillip W. Not sure but I will try and post one on here in a min of one I have saved to my flash drive.

David W. My father worked in the Road Vehicle Shop in the Works 1934-1971.

Gary C. We made toilet roll holders, towel rails, mug racks, chess boards, pool cues, window frames, fishing tackle boxes............. the trick was getting them out .

Chris G. Chuck and catch over the Blackboards Gary

Gary C. Yeah tried that but the buggers that walked their dogs along the tow path got wise to that and nicked it before you got out of work.

David W. My Dad used to be a wood machinist, chaps would come to see him in the morning and ask "any chance of a scrap piece of teak or mahogany Jack ". He would ask, "what size do you wants? OK leave it with me, come back around 4.00pm and I will see what I can find. They would then collect their request plus the "chitty" saying it was scrap wood of nil value to take out that evening!

Bryan D. Those were the days! My Dad once brought me home a kaleidoscope that either he made or got someone else to make. The only thing it lacked was a "made in Wolverton Works" label.

Chris G. They caught a load of lads in my era making weightlifting equipment and taking it out bit by bit, I kid you not.

Ivor S. My dad made his allotment shed out of the "Trek Cart" they were allowed to take home. Probably why all the sheds up the allotments looked the same.

Danny K. And they all shook when the works hooter went off.

Ivor S. That hooter was more reliable than Big Ben!

Phillip W. You don't hear it much any more.

Clive T. I made a set of weight bars for squats and if you had a motorbike the best friend was in the plating shop for chroming - think it was Aubrey Townsend? Exhausts were stripped off in your tea break and reassembled to ride home on.

Steve A. Duffle bags were made in the trim shop and just by

chance they were the perfect diameter to fit a 5ltr tin of glue into.
Jackie N. Some of the wood block flooring is left at Moon Street
School, though most of it is covered by carpet now. What's left will
have been polished during the holidays and will look lovely........?

Central Cafe

Bryan D. We were talking the other day about the Central Cafe.
Well this photo show what those four buildings looked like in
1957. Past the Post Office you have the Central cafe, then a private
house, the Leigh the Chemist, then Brighton bakery on the corner.
The Chemist was taken over by Taylors - now Tandoori.
The occasion of this photo was a fund raising effort by TocH, once
a thriving men's organization in Wolverton. they used to meet in
that building behind the Palace and their sign was an Aladdin's
lamp.

Toc H Fundraisers 1957

Sheila S Am I right that the Central Cafe was originally owned
by Easts?
Bryan D I think so. Cyril East was the baker and Ken his son. I
think it was Ken's wife who ran the cafe. As teenagers we used to
go in on Saturday mornings for a cup of tea in the back room. We
must have thought we were terribly grown up and Mrs East was
highly amused.
Sheila S I remember the daughter Sheila East, don't know what
happened to her do you?
Brian E I do know Ken East (who drove for Johnsons' Coaches
of Hanslope) had The Central Cafe after the Taylors. Ken drove a

maroon Humber Hawk. I don't know who Cyril was. Maybe, the Taylors rented the cafe of the Easts for a period?

Cuppa Tea

Ian H. Just made the good lady a cup of tea (thé noir au citron) and it got me thinking about those old fragile brown tea-pots. The spouts came in for some hard times and often parts were broken off................not to worry just slip on one of those red rubber flexible spouts! What about tea cosies too, anyone still got them. Tea-bags phooff!!!

Ruth E. Aah welcome back Ian xx I have succumbed to tea bags but always make my tea in a pot with a cosy. I have two, for a small and large pot. Not seen those red spouts for years but sure someone on here will find one lol...

Bryan D. You have a great memory for those little details Ian. I wonder why tea cosies disappeared?

Brian E. I recently stopped using tea-bags and reverted back to leaves. And, I managed to find a white 2/3 cup tea-pot with it's own integrated, padded cosy. It is brilliant, and of course it holds the lid on as well. I found it in the Willen Hospice shop at Bletchley! I use the tea-leaves for the garden.

Pete B. I have an old teapot strapped to a treatrunk for a birdbox .

Ian H. PG Tits Pete!!

Pat B. The tea cosy has not disappeared, I have one. You would most likely get one in Maisies or a craft fair.

Sharon Sherwood I prefer leaves and have a red knitted cosy
Sharon Sherwood They sell knitting patterns for them

Bryan D. After I wrote about the disappearance of the tea cosy yesterday I checked around and as Pat and Sharon have testified they have not disappeared. They've just disappeared from my house, which is a different matter altogether.

Pat C. Was looking at a selection in a shop window on Saturday they caught my eye becuse i thought they were obsolete must be old stock. Ours were always handknits.

Brian E. Yes, Pat, they were always knitted, not bought!

Ron B. I bet there is not a man on here, that when left in a room on his own, has not tried on the tea cosy

Ian H. That has made me laugh out loud Ron :-)

Ron B. I know I have Ian. Can't resist.

Sheila M. [:-|

Brian E. If, like me, you use tea-leaves, try South Indian Mamri. I found it on eBay and it is delicious.

Ian H. Just changing caffeine for a minute..................I love grinding coffee and the smell, better than the taste almost.

Sarah K. I've got a teacosy in the shape of a black sheep - I liked it the minute I saw it! My Auntie Daphne uswed to use loose tea she had one of those dispensers that measured it for you

June L. I've got 3 dark brown glaze teapots all different sizes, the smallest is a 1 cup size. They are known as Brown Betty Teapots & said to make the Best cuppa & the Pots keep the tea hottest longer.

Ron B. Is that Bra or tea June? lol

Bev P. I collect teapots. When I was home I wanted to buy a knitted cozy so badly. The only cozy I found was at the shops at Windsor station, it's hard to describe how they made it. I've seen knitted ones on ebay, also patterns but never tried to make my own.

Toni B. What about antimacassar, those cloth protections used on the backs of chairs. I knwo we had them.

Penny G. You can still buy those antimacassers Toni.

Toni B. Ha ha, Penny. I've got leather so just give it a wipe now and then.

Brian E. Not just the backs of chairs, we had shaped things that fitted over the end of the arms.

First job

Becca H. Just wondering what other Wolvertonians did for their first 'real' job. When I left school in 73 it was very easy to get a job - and lots of temp opportunities too. My first 'real' pay packet came from Copperads in Old Woverton. I also remember quite a few girls in the years above me going to Rode Coats near Bletchley. Some also went into the print. I remember thinking I was so well off when my pay went UP to £16 A WEEK!

Lesley W. Trainee Dental nurse ..long time ago £12 odd a week .

Chris G. Twenty odd quid, Works apprentice 1978, more money than we knew what to do with, that soon changed...I went in the Works for five years to do an apprenticeship, but you couldn't really describe that as a proper job, it was just an extension of school but with bigger kids. No homework, playtime was much longer and instead of school dinners you went to the pub. Happy days. Oh and I think they paid us too...

Pat B. Wolverton Works Accounts Office. 1956. £2.19s.6p. a week.

Ian H. Electronics engineer Plessey at Towcester. Disaster!!

Deborah B. My first job was in Wolverton Works in 1978/79. Was in the typist office - manual typewriters. Think was about £375/

month. Betty was my boss.

Deborah C. Secretarial apprentice at Associated Octel in Bletchley - very nice people!

Edith H. Barclays Bank, Stationery Office, London, then back to Bletchley.

Gareth G. Apprentice panel beater at Millbay Transport on Old Wolverton Road 1968 I Was on about 7 quid a week. Remember saving up for my first Crombie (£20) Ben Sherman (£5) and Levi's (£5) in 1969/70 on 9 quid a week with a bit of help from my mum - about £25 ;-)I worked with Chris Berry at Millbay, can't remember if he was made redundant from Aston's or just left but he came to Millbay in 1970 or 1971 when I was an apprentice. Regarding the Aston Martin story: The director of Millbay had a new Aston delivered to Millbay awaiting registration, I couldn't wait to have my picture taken with it, so I sat on the front posing while someone took the photo. Unfortunately where I sat (right on the badge) is a weak point and my bum put a dent in the panel. Luckily Chris saved me from the sack by knowing exactly where to push to get the dent out invisibly, which he did promptly without the boss finding out. Phew!!!! Nice

David O. Apprentice in the works about a fiver a week 1968.

Sheila B. Wolverton Library. How did I manage?

Ian S. Becca I did 4 years at Copperads 78 to 82.

Brian E. Stanley Wood Reproduction Furniture Ltd. at Newport Pagnall. I was a wages clerk on £7 a week.

Julia B. East Midlands Electricity Board. Started 1973. Have a pay slip dated 25th Oct 1974, £70.69. Mother Bennett took £20.00 board and lodging which unbeknownst to me she was saving towards me wedding. Ha-ha, still saving then

Andy C. Wolverton Works 1976 along with about 16 other trainee office bods. £17 a week while on emergency tax code of which my " keep" was taken by Mum and Dad leaving me £7 a week to spend illegally in either the "snug" of the Vic in Wolverton or The Craufurd.

Elaine S. BHRA - British Hydromechanics Research Assoc. at Cranfield in the library - 1966 £6 15s a week.

Graham S. Bricklayer apprentice £ 25. a week. 78/79

Alan C. Lloyds Bank Wolverton 1962 £28 pounds a month.

Steve A. I've managed to avoid a real job for the last 30yrs, but I attended the works from the age of 16 to 24.

Edward Q. Apprentice with British rail eng. 1961.

Julie W. Budgens on the square, £28 a week to start with in 1985 xx

Jennifer T. Co-op offices above the Co-op bank, wages £2.15s (£2. 75p) Sheila Stone worked there too. I left Moon St school Christmas 1960 aged 15, I then went to work in the Co-op offices above the Co-op Bank on the square, the wage was £2 ... 15 shilling per week, to start we had to sort out the divi stubs, and count the milk tokens that the milk men bought in every day as well as making tea for the whole office.

Geoff L. Apprentice Wolverton Works 1957 then royal navy in 1958.

Jane B. 1977 - Copy Typist - Telephone Rentals - Bletchley - £19 per week take home pay !!!!

Gill B. I also worked at the Co-op offices on the square and later in the bank downstairs until 1968. I think when I started in 1963 the starting wage was £3. 14s per week.

Hazel S. I lasted a month in the check office at the Co-op 1959. Sat in there with Maud made the tea also for the rest of the offices downstairs.

Marc H. First job as a floor layer for an old boy up Towcester wish I had stuck at that £13.56 gave that up after a year for an extra £2 per week cutting trees down(lumberjack) I think they called it. I had the opportunity to go in the works or Print and Plessey.

Susan H. Supernumerary Clerical Trainee in the Works in 1970. Worked in all of the offices for about two weeks each. I earned the princely sum if £12 a week.

Sylvia A. First job after leaving school was in Macaras delicatessen in Bletchley. If I remember correctly I had to get the number 44 bus. before the dial a bus came in.

Pete B. My first job was at the boat yard Cosgrove,£8.23p a week, hated it so became a co op milkman £15 age 17 then up £50 age 18(mans wage) Hated it .2 days at Rocla pipes .hated it. 4 months in BR ,hated it. Then became a motorbike mechanic . LOVE IT !!!

Shell F. I worked at the Agora helping doing the indoor market

Helen P. I worked round the old road with my Dad and my Uncle Frankie at the mill.

Kim P. Becca, apparently laundrettes haven't changed much then! My first full time job was at Milton Keynes Library, it was pretty new then, first in the lending library then reference. I was there about five years. While I was still at school I worked at the Bull Hotel in Stony for about nine months, I was the Saturday/Sunday chambermaid, Mo Dackombe was the weekday housekeeper, she got me the job. Then I was at Terry's for a while... less said about that the better lol. Kay and I didn't get on very well!

Susan H. Whilst still at school and in further education I worked for Taylor's Cafe and outside caterers which helped with my train fare from Wolverton to Bletchley and paid for my books etc. My first full time job was with GEC Avionics on Standing way in 1986 (I think) Wages were £56 per week. Happy Days!!

Clare M. My first job was at the works, £45 a week. I think I was better off then than I am now! At least if I'd spent it all by

Wednesday I knew Friday's pay day wasn't far off :)

Becca H. Before I left school I did a couple of catering shifts for a firm that was based in a cafe in Bletchley. I was meant to be just a 'washer upper' - However, on my second (and last!) shift one of the waitresses had gone off sick and I had to (unwisely) step into the breach. The boss gave me a bit of a briefing whilst the older ladies fussed about putting a white blouse and skirt on me (size 14 and I was a small 8) Anyways, it was a posh do and I was finally ready to make my waitressing debut. Starting me of "at the shallow end" I was given the job of serving tartare sauce - asking each of the posh diners individually "excuse me sir / madam, would you like tartare sauce?" Sounds simple enough don't it? Well it seemed to be going well till some Hooray Henry blokes started taking the p*** out my oversized and ill fitting outside. I tried to ignore them , but got myself a tad flummoxed - then turned to the next lady bountiful - and heard myself say " excuse me madam would you like some tortoise arse! - She complained loudly - I got sacked and had to walk home from Cosgrove on my own. Happy Days ??? (But I have dined out on the story a few times over the last 4 decades! x

Sheila S. My first job was typist at Keen Shay Keens (accountants) in Stony, wage was £3 per week!!!

Ruth E. My first job was at Pearks the Grocers for a princely sum of £4.2/6p .....1965, where I was taught to use one of those old red bacon slicers, bone sides of bacon and tie up for joints, cut up 60lb cheeses the correct way (woe betide if it was wrong and some old dear got all rind)!weigh all our loose biscuits, lard,fruit,cherries. No Elf and Safety then !!!!

Alan Cr. Apprentice electrician for G.F.Gray and Sons Ltd, Fenny Stratford. 9 quid a week.......

Terry L. Co-op Braddle High street £16 a week and as many dead mice as you could eat !

Angie A. My first job was at Bletchley Urban District Council, Victoria Rd, Bletchley, writing out job tickets for the plumbers and electricians, brickies etc.. Don't remember what my wages were, however I do recall having a savings account in the Trustee Savings Bank on the Square and used to have a little book recording all my deposits. Thought I was the bees knees.

John R. My first real job, aside from paper rounds and washing dishes at the M1 cafe, was an apprentice at Hanslope Park. That lasted about 6 months, I ended up being really bored so I quit and went and joined the Army. In hindsight, a really smart move.

Richie B. My 1st job was Kentwood's on Glyn square loved it.

Ian B. Had two jobs to choose from trainee with GPO or BT as it is these days or trainee at Hanslope Park chose Hanslope Park

£7.00 a week.

Pina R. 1st proper full time job was at City of Westminster Assurance, CMK, about £120 per month if I remember correctly, 1980. Prior to that worked in Waitrose (£8 per weekend) also helped out occasionally at a jewellers in Bletchley during school hols etc....

Jill G. I was 16 and I worked for Beclawatt Newport Pagnell making tensa barriers, the spring loaded barriers - you see them everywhere banks, shops, airports, I worked there right up to having my son George I was 24. £16 a week.

Susan B. My first job was working in the McCorquodales from 1975 to 1978 and I was 15 yrs

Brian E. Stanley Wood Reproductions Ltd. Newport Pagnall. Wages Clerk at seven quid a week!

Susan B. Steve's dad worked there Jill as well, was he there the same time as you before he was made redundant.

Jill G. Yes he was there when I was Sue.

June L. I was 15 & because my mum was a trained seamstress in Oxford St London W1 she whisked me off to Old St in London to become a Tailoress. I had a journey of 11/2 hours to work & back again each day. I caught a train at 6.30 in the morning & got home at 7o'clock in the eve, I was so tired. My wage was £2 10 shillings per week

Lynette M. I worked Dunlop and Rankin for £17 a wk 1976-81.

Susan B. Was that on the Old Wolverton Rd, as Steve recalls his dad working there too.

Lynette M. Did you mean Dunlop + Rankin Susan? If so, no. Glyn square back of houses in St Georges Way.

Susan B. I will have to ask father in law Lynette. Steve's first job was at old Stratford at a factory on the corner of the Deanshanger Rd opposite the white swan being paid £4 a week in 1970.

Lynette M. Yes I know where that is or was by the Swan pub my husbands aunt and uncle ran the swan yrs ago.

Janice M. Julies pantry.

Marc H. Mine was a floor layer first weeks wage £13.56 think I may still have my wage slip somewhere.

Elaine H. BHRA - British Hydromechanics Research Assoc at Cranfield. £6 15s a week.

Len E. Brown Bothers Ltd, Old Woverton 1975, £25.00 pw, thought it a lot of money for a 16 year old.

June L. Susan do you mean Druces on the corner? If you do, my husband Peter Levitt & your father in law are sure to know each other, what's his name, was he in Fabrication?

Geoffrey W. Thompson's the accountants at Stony Stratford, £3.00 a week.

Jane B. Copy Typist at Telephone Rentals, Bletchley - £19 per week !!!

Susan B. His name is Harold, his brother Ron still lives in Buckingham St

Janet S. I worked in Pearks on the Stratford road, Hilda Brown was the manageress I got £3 9/6 that was 1964

June L. What is his Surname Susan?

Jill G. June I am sure Sue wont mind me saying his surname is Blackwell.

Ralph C. Desouter bros in Colindale London as an apprentice 27 pound a week

Pamela J. 15 and I went into Wolverton Works Offices

Lin G. Copy typist in typing pool, Wolverton Works aged 16, I'm amazed people remember how much they earned as I can't.

Pat C. TSB Aylesbury 1961 £4.4s.0p plus 3s.6p per week for late night on Friday 6pm.

Deborah B. Copy typist in typing pool 1978 aged 18. Wages? can't remember either Lin.

Pam F. 1963 I was 17 started in the Print (McCorqudales)

Vivienne B. Associated Octel Ltd, Bletchley. Accounts Office 1970 £20 a week,

Phillip W. Lyon house ltd kiln farm in 1997 not long after my 18 the birthday as stayed on Radcliffe for an extra year.

Wendy C. Snuggle Down Of Norway Kiln Farm.

Bryan D. March 1959. Left school to work at Ministry of Pensions and National Insurance where I checked Ni stamps. Pretty easy work for £5 a week.

Keith T. Coop in church St 1970 £8 per week

Geoff L. BR training school aged 15 in 1957

Brian L. Red cross Old Wolverton YTS.

Andrew B. Comet Northampton, whilst I waited to join Navy in 1981.

Tricia D. I joined Budgen - even remember my first interview 'Mr ....., when I leave school can I work here?' - "Yes okay Patricia." - sorted! If only all jobs were so easy.....

John Rd. MacDonald's at 16. didn't last long though

Tricia D. I think I got £8.72 Not sure if that was a week or thurs/ fri-Sat! used to give mum £5.....and still had loads left.....

I used to give extra cheese/ham etc and nicer bacon - if someone asked for cheap bacon I'd charge the cheap price but give them back bacon ..... that's why they never made any money and..... if people with money came in - I'd mostly always - add extra so if they wanted 8ozs cheese - I'd serve 10-12ozs. Oh! it's alright.... my version of Robin Hood.

Helen F. I left at 16 and went to a YTS in Kiln Farm.

Deborah C. Secretarial Apprentice at Associated Octel in Bletchley - just 16! x

Vivienne B. Deborah Creedy I worked at Associated Octel Junior Accounts Clerk I was just 15 in 1970, I was there when we went decimal. Did Jenny Hawkins work there when you did? she is a Wolverton person.

Deborah C. Vivienne - I worked at Octel from 1980 to 81/2. Name doesn't ring a bell but then it WAS a long time ago! I loved it there but it was only a two year thing so then went and worked as Office Manager at Hoist Mec forklifts down the road! xx

Jane D. The Co-op in the Agora on a YTS training scheme at 16. Ended up there for 13 years.

Dale B. Halfords in Queensway, Bletchley at 17yrs & working on the H4 V6 Building site at 16yrs called Scott Hales. One of the first Bridge pours, was the Foot bridge after the Canal Bridge, leading towards the City we know now. Joined the Army at 18yrs & first posting was Hong Kong. Good times..!!

Andy M. Joined the Army, The Life Guards, in 1967. Enjoyed so much, I stayed for 25 years!

Susan K. Not really my first official job, but I spent many hours after school and during school holidays stacking shelves in Budgens on the Square while waiting for my Mum to finish work!

Vince C. Wolverton Motor Company, on the hire cars/vans as Valeter. Worked there before I went on to do IT course at MK College.

Ingrid M. Ida ??? was my manager. Then I got a job at the Senior Nursing Home in Newport. Anyone remember that place.. Depressing as all hell. Is it still there?

Brian E. Renny Lodge, Ingrid? I remember Mr Irani from my weekend job at Blue Star on the M1

Jane Br. My first paid job was at Blow Mocan, Kiln Farm, Summer 83.

Only a Few

Ian H. Only a few of the lads of my generation went in the army or navy etc. Our poster Geoff Labrum of course leads the list being a member of the Royal Navy, Tony Hobson, much to the surprise of many, signed up for the Army and did about 9 years, I believe Freddie Buckingham did too, Dave Hobson, Tony's brother spent two or three in the Merchant Navy, Pete Birchenough joined the police and there was a lad who had an earring that lived up the top end of Windsor St(he hailed from New Bradwell) who also spent some time in the Merchant Navy and I can't think beyond that............not many considering the size of the population. Was it the same in the next generation?

Brian E. When I was at school - early sixties - a few joined the forces. Most of course went into The Works. I was one of the few boys who didn't back then. A particular friend of mine then, Edward Briggs, joined the army, and was killed shortly after in NI. A great shock to me at the time, and I still have sad memories of that.

Ian H. That reminds me Brian one of the English boys from Anson Road? was crippled whilst serving in the Army in Malaya, as it was called, he was a few years older than me probably born mid 1930's.

Andy M. I was in the Household Cavalry, The Life Guards, for 25 years. Enjoyed every minute.

John R. I figured out I didn't want to go into the Works fairly early on, so after a brief stint as an apprentice at Hanslope Park, I joined the Army (Royal Signals) for 6 years. Overall, had a good time and got to see a bit of the world.

Brian E. Andy, did you know Edward Briggs? They lived at Pineham, just along the road from yours, Castlethorpe corner?

Becca H. It was partly the fault of the two Gleadell kids from across the road in Woodland View that John (Robbo) joined the Army - hehehe!

Ian H. Geoff Smith also, he went into the RAF and maybe Brian Eldred went in the army or it could have been the TA for him Which years Andy ?

Bryan D. There was still the shadow of National Service hanging over us and there was the memory of the war in our parents mind so I suspect that service in the forces may have been discouraged. In any case, as the 60s dawned there was full employment and military pay was not that good.

Stan B. Of my 2 years National Service in the Army, I spent 19months in Hong Kong.

Ian H. My brother Reg signed on for an extra year Stan (something to do with more money I think) out of his 3 years two and a half were spent in Libya, he went to Malta for regulatory holidays his N° 23214345

Bryan D. Were we the first year not to get called up for NS Ian? They were still conscripting up to 1960 I believe, but none of my year (as far as I know) ever got the call.

Ian H. Think we missed by two years Bryan

Hazel S. I know of people born in 1940 who missed National Service.

Bryan D. Probably right. I remember Tony Little and Des Whiteside had to do their time but after that they must have relaxed the rules. Technically we were eligible but I think they were winding down .

Brian E. Had there still been conscription then Bryan, we would have no Beatles.

Pat B. I Think Stan b.1939 was the part of the last but one intake.

Ian H. Eric my other brother did conscription, in the R.E.M.E his n° was 22902183

Peter L. 23437419 Gdsm Levitt, P my two year's were very interesting.

Ian H. I seem to think Ron Stones (Furze Way) went in the Royal Navy? Peter how do you think the" number" was calculated, your's and my brothers' are in the millions so I doubt it is simply additional?

Foreigners

Ian H. As a child the population make-up in Wolverton was a lot different to how it was when I last visited about 4years ago. From memory I will give a list of those I knew and were not British in the 40/50's.Mrs Morgan who lived on the Square she was French, her children had "French" names Hubert, Bernard and Marie. Mrs Berry, think she was Maltese lived in Furze Way. There was another French lady too she lived opposite the Nimmo family in Windsor St they didn't have children. One of the Neale's married a South African Lady, her son was Geoff Llewellyn. Mr Llewellyn and Miss Robottom who were teachers, I believe he was Anglo Indian and she West Indian. There was a Polish man who lived down Furze Way who was married to an English girl and two doors away from the Scout Hall lived an Irish man who you could sometimes hear play his flute. The Gills, Indian, (Clarence lived diagonally opposite Bryan D.) came in the 50's Pete I understand is in France There were others..........!!

Of course we mustn't forget the Sicilian who had the chippy later on and the Greek barber down the hill. That's about it, amazing eh??

Ruth E. Viv Berry was my mother in law and was indeed Maltese the Polish man in Furze way was married to Beryl Faulkner who had a son John who was a policeman, funny tale about him I might post later in his capacity as a policeman! I lived next door to the Gills in Victoria St! Nana Gill helped with my Cathocism lessons before marrying Chris Berry ,there were 6 Gills I believe ,Clarence, Rita, Merle, Michael Peter,Dougie. Nearly all settled in Wolverton apart from Peter and Dougie.

Ian H. Ruth, I remember now, also I remember John a good looking fella if my memory serves me right.

Anthony Z. Kowalski's in Furze way, son Andy step brother to John Faulkner Det Inspector.

Vicki L. Yes Pina I knew Liz & on FB with her!! I know her mum is Italian. :) It was funny when I used to see her & your mum talking very loudly in that lovely Italian way!! Know john (chippy) in my class!! Forgot to mention them. Happy days remembering the entire folk x

Ruth E. Yes that would be him he must be retired by now I think... Oh there was also Maisie Phillips from Southern Way not sure what nationality had 2 girls

Pina R. I remember the Polish guy on Furze Way, forgot his name now, my Dad (Polish) knew him. Maybe Anthony Zastawny might remember him? There were quite a few Polish blokes living in Wolverton also there was quite a few Italians.... (My Mum!)

Ian H. Who, when and where Pina? I can't recall them in my childhood, late 40's, that is except those I've mentioned, your mum and dad for example (without being impertinent of course)

Vicki L. The North's were from Gibraltar & lived in Furze way ~ Julie McGee's grandparents were Italian in Buckingham St. Shelpa & family were Indian also Buckingham St. Liz Zavrick (spelt wrong!!!) Parent polish lived ??? Great days meeting different cultures as a child x

Pina R. My Dad moved into Anson Rd late 50s or 1960. They got married in 62 so Mum moved to Wolverton then. Vicki, its Liz Szafryk you mean, she has a sister Teresa, my age, and I grew up with them. My mum & theirs are from the same village in Italy & they both worked & lived in Leeds before moving to Wolverton when they married. 2 Italians married 2 Polish blokes! Other Italians were the Agostinellis' on Osborne St, Iorizzos' on Peel Rd, Cosenza's' on Church St, Miceli (chippy) on Cambridge St, then there were the Greco's', Buscaglias' but don't know when they all moved in. There was a Polish guy known as little Stanley on Anson Rd as well as Anthony Zastawny dad. Also Charlie Wojcik but can't remember where he lived, think top end Wolverton. Can't think of any others at the moment.

Bryan D. I'm with you Ian. Wolverton has always been open to all comers. You mentioned Graham Camozzi the other day. Well his ancestor came from Italy in the early 1800s and Lewis (or Luigi) Camozzi was one of new Wolverton's earliest residents. In fact the Camozzi credentials go back further than most of us as Wolvertonians.

Margaret C. Mrs Gill was a lovely lady she lived next door to Dick and Sylvia Russell in Victoria Street.

Ian H. I'd forgotten to mention the Cammozzi family Bryan , any news of Joe?

Bryan D. Don't know. I never had much to do with the Camozzis. Graham was a year or two older and Royston, who was in our year through junior school seemed to move in other circles.

Ian H. I believe one of the reasons a few Polish and Italian families came to Wolverton was because of the relatively close proximity of the brick industry and Bedford in particular.IT was home to immigrants just after the war men who were more than happy to do this hard work. Later of course the West Indians came to Bedford in large numbers. Perhaps these people wrote home to brothers and sisters to say that Wolverton was good place for work and to live.

Ian H. There was Brian too who was the same age as my late sister Née 1932

Pina R. My Dad came over during the war.....he then lived in a hostel in Wing & then in Bletchley if I remember correctly. He worked as a trackman for British Rail. Then he lodged for a short while with @Anthony Zastawnys parents in Anson Rd & when no 66 came up for sale he bought it.

Alan C. I believe Dr Delahunty was Irish. The Mr Llewellyn mentioned was a teacher his name was Roy and he taught at the Secondary Modern School, he was an excellent field hockey player. He was at the Secondary Modern School on Aylesbury Street at the same time as Bob Dunleavy.

Ian H. Alan I can still hear his wonderful Irish brogue, thanks for that. I believe I mentioned him on an earlier topic, it's the "head" you see, not what it was.

Alan C. Ian yes he made house calls as well most of the younger people on this site probably do not know what they are!!!!!!

Ian H. He didn't deliver me that was Dr Lowry? His predecessor. My mother said she gave me a Scottish forename in deference to him!!

Bryan D. Lowry rings no bells. There was a Dr David Max at Yiewsley prior to Delahunty. Dr Lawrence practised on the Stratford Rd.

Ian H. Could be Lawrence then Bryan, I was a bit too young to remember.

Alan Co. Bryan where did Dr Lawrence practice on the Stratford Rd?

Ruth E. There was a surgery in Stratford rd. near Riteprice I think

Bryan D. Number 37. It now appears to be a private house. The dental practice next door at No. 36 with a bay window is still going. Used to be Montague Watts.

Chris G. Monty Watts, the mention of the name sends shivers down quite a few spines I'm sure. The Mr Magoo of the dentistry world.

Ian H. Went there Bryan! Broke my front teeth going over the handlebars down the station hill. Geoff Woodward was with me, my mother was not pleased.

Chris G. I'm Bucks born and bred (yep thick arm, thick head) but our Dad was a Falkland Islander, came 8,000 miles to the UK in

WWII and never went back, funnily enough the old North Bucks accent is not dissimilar so he probably had a smoother path than most.

Ian H. Now I may be wrong Pina but something at the back of my mind tells me that Italian soldiers were held in a detention camp along the Old Wolverton Rd during and after the war for a while?

Margaret C. That's what my Mum told me Ian that the POW's worked alongside her in Tilley's Woodyard..

Vicky L. How could I have forgotten Rosetta :)? At her house, we swung on the washing line & it broke :) 3 of us went down, 2 broke their arms, I didn't and was as jealous as I wanted a cast!!!!

Chris G. Worked in the Works on the oxycutters with a little Polish guy from Cambridge St, the name Witowski rings a bell, maybe Johnny Witowski, though of course it could be something completely different. Worked on Geoff Beales gang.

Margaret C. I think there was a Polish man that lived in the Gables early 70's think name was Patynik, prob spelt that wrong he had 2 daughters, lived on the 5th floor opposite corner to myself..

Pina R. Margaret C. , yes his names Stefan, he now lives in the place next to the gables, forgot its name now. Ian H., you may be right about the Italian soldiers, I don't know. My Dad was a Polish prisoner of war!

Ian H. I've got a photo of a great Pole in my "office" he had a big job in Rome!!

Margaret C. The place next to the Gables is a sheltered housing called Orchard House. Do you know what become of his 2 girls I think the eldest was Joan. Think the POW's my Mum spoke about were Polish.

Pina R. Ian H., my Dad looked a lot like that 'Pole' who lived in Rome. The year he became Pope, we holidayed in Mums hometown. She went round telling the locals that He & Dad were related! She never did go to confession, not that I know of anyway, lol! Margaret C. , Stefan is a friend of mums, they keep in touch. One daughter is named Yanina & can't think of the other daughters name right now. One of them lives in Northampton. Mum visited Stefan when we were in the UK earlier in the year. Couldn't think of the name Orchard House before!

Chris G. Yep Stefan still alive and well, my Mum was in Orchard House till a couple of months back and Stefan was the life and soul of the place, doing a lot of things for the other pensioners there.

Pina R. Thinking about it, Charlie Wojcik may have also lived at The Gables.

Ian H. What I find telling about this thread is how these "foreigners" fitted in to the community and were liked, known and respected. Today's young probably don't know a thing about the overseas people who have arrived in Wolverton, and they probably are less likely to integrate. Pretty much the same anywhere in the UK now. France is a little more tolerant in this respect however there are still huge problems in the "cities" of the big conurbations.

Bryan D. It's a serious point Ian. The great thing about the Wolverton we knew, and the generation after us knew, was that everybody in Wolverton understood what Wolverton was about, so newcomers could be quickly integrated into the community if they so wished. Someone put up a cricket photo a few days ago with Leo Bostock standing there in his umpire's smock. I do recall when those Lancashire people came down to Wolverton after they closed Newton Heath there was some initial suspicion. There were silly jokes, for example, about them keeping coal in the bath. But Leo Bostock, who was a good teller of jokes himself, quickly integrated - as they all did. Going back to 1840 you would be hard pressed to find a single Roman Catholic in Wolverton, but they came and had to trudge the 10 miles to Weston Underwood for Mass. In time they built their own church within the community and became fully functioning members of the community. But, as you say, times have changed, and people are less attached to the community where they live.

Ian S. I bet you could not name them now

Ian H. Precisely my point Ian ,alas.

Ian H. Bryan I have spoken to my two elder brothers today. The name of the doctor was Irvin(e.g.)

Bryan D. Hmm! So you could have been named Irvine Hickson! :)

Kim P. There was a lady named Dolly from Barbados who lived somewhere around Victoria Street in the early 70's, she and her husband Ricky who I think was Jamaican had been there a good few years by then but that's when we got to know them. Dolly and my mum were very close friends, she was always "aunt Dolly" to me. She made my mum laugh so hard one time, probably around 1977/8, she got up a petition against a proposed Indian takeaway because she said "We don't want any of those w*** round here"!

Galleon Estate

Tony K. Don't know if this has been discussed before, so apologies if it has. My sister Sue Whitehead and I grew up on the Galleon estate, but spent a lot of time in the streets of Wolverton as that is where most of our friends lived. Our parents (Jean and John Kay) moved to the Galleon estate from London when it was first built (Around 1965). Anyway, does anyone remember it being built? What was the reaction from the local community etc? Will post some pics when I have dug them out.

Terry L. Remember it being built, no reaction on my part as only six years old, but later years some of us thought that people who moved from the Old Town to the Galleon were a bit, how shall we say this, Hmm going middle class, Blue to white collar. But then my mate moved there and bought the tone right down and I realised it was just an extension to Wolverton

Janet B. Ha ha Terry that's what one of my friends said to me, that we were getting Posh! I told her living in a new built house didn't make me a different person, nor did it. Used to walk over every Thursday night to see how it was progressing.

When we put our deposit down we were told it would be ready for November, it wasnt finished till March. We moved in the day I came out of the Barratt, the boys being nine days old. Never did things by half!!! LOL

Bryan D. I recall it being built and was the first new build since Southern Way. By this time terraced housing was out of fashion - although MK did build those chicken coops at Fullers Slade. I don't recall anybody being against it.

 Old Wolverton had a tiny population back then, most of whom lived in Slated Row or Manor Farm Cottages, so if there was any objection it may not have been heard. It was a conventional sixties development. When the Milton Keynes architects got going at Galley Hill and Fullers Slade, then you started to hear some puzzled comments.

Toni B. I remember it being referred to as those posh new houses. My uncle lived in Newport Pagnell in a house very like the Galleon one's little Linford lane up by the M1 services. He brought new in the early 60's. Janet, can you remember the sale prices?

Bryan D. I worked as a labourer on those houses by the M1, probably in 1961. I'm surprised they're still standing!

Bernice T

It started with houses built by Wren Homes who went out of business then Trinity Road came - was that Wimpey Janet? - the next phase included Caxton Road and I moved there in 1965 - last phase was Longville- these were the fields where the Co-op horses were grazed - I remember we made sure we put Old Wolverton in the address - was that snobbish ha ha !!!!

Toni B. My uncle died a few years ago, I loved his house surprisingly good size inside. Even in his garden the motorway is not THAT noisy.

Chris G. I can remember people from Old Wolverton not drinking their tea out the saucer.

Andrew L. It was always an aspiration for my elders, when I was growing up in the terraces, to escape to either Galleon Estate or to Haversham. Don't know when Rowan Ave, Chalmers Ave were built, must be about the same time. Now years later here I am living in a 1960s build house.

Jane B. When we moved here in 1966 my Mum and Dad were going to buy a house in Caxton Road - but then the EMEB who Dad worked for offered us a house in Victoria Street - and Mum is still there!!!!

Ian H. It can't have been posh, my brother Eric lived there! It was certainly a refreshing development, adding to the class of Wolverton and its inhabitants

Julie M. Moved to the galleon estate in 1966 just before my 2nd birthday but remember the workmen building the houses over the road as it was built by 2 different companies must have been about 4 when it was finished think Longville was the last to be finished though but then I was small lol

Jackie N. Tony, I think you lived at the bottom of my Mum and Dad's garden (if you know what I mean!)-they lived at 66 Trinity Road from 1971 (Mr and Mrs Tite)

Janet B. Toni we paid three thousand and sixty-five for ours. We had to pay a little extra as it was on a corner, with a little more land. This was 1966 as Bernice has said Longville was the last road to be built, after living there for a year the other side backing on to the canal was built.

Toni B. Janet. .. bet it worried you all that borrowed .loll

Ian H. Phew!!!!! Janet, I thought you were really really rich! X

Janet B. Gave me fright when I saw what I had written Ian, no I'm not Rothschild!!! x

Tony K. Hells bells Jackie! I do remember the Tite family and yes you were at the bottom of our garden, number 54. I was born in 1971. How are you? My parents paid around 3k for their house as well. Found all of the details when they sadly passed away.

Janet B. Bernice, yes it was Wimpey that took over after Wren Homes went out of business. The last houses to be built were at the back of me where building material was kept. This was numbers 1 to 7 Manor Rd.

Tony K. Does anybody remember the Moody family from Trinity road, would have been in the 70's. I used to be good friends with Simon Moody; he lived next door to Jason Sheen. The 3 of us used to play on what was then the little playing field.

Andrew L. I remember Simon Moody, and Sharon Sheen.

Ian B. It was started before 65. There were several houses built along the Old Wolverton Road first. I used to deliver papers to them in 1963.

Jackie N. Tony, I'm fine -live at Blue Bridge. Mum and Dad both now passed away, sadly -they really enjoyed living in Trinity Road -as various people have said, thought they'd really "arrived"

by moving over to Old Wolverton ! (From Oxford Street) Dad particularly liked having more garden over there.

Kim P. I remember the Moody's and the Sheens, mostly through school though. I used to come over to see Debi at number 6 but that was when we were a bit older I think. Sorry to hear about your mum and dad Tony.

Karen T. Hi Tony, my parents are still on the Galleon estate but I'm afraid I don't know a great deal about its history. I'll ask them. How are you?

Brenda C. I moved to the Galleon Estate when I was 13 in 1963. We had one of the first houses built. My dad paid £2500, sounds ridiculous now but was a lot of money then.

Sue W. I wish I could remember surnames as I would ask if people knew or remembered friends I had from the estate..... Just a point though... Definitely not posh x

Maggie S. I remember my Dad working on the building of the Galleon Estate, I think he worked for a firm called Green & Cody. They also built the telephone exchange by Creed St.

Kim P. The Galleon Estate was one of the last (if not THE last) Wolverton developments before MKDC moved in. We came to Wolverton because my dad was offered the chance to get in on the ground floor with MKDC which came together in 1969. Galleon IMO has the kudos of being "real" Wolverton whereas Greenleys, Stacey Bushes etc. don't quite make it

Bryan D. I know what you mean by "real Wolverton" but Greenleys was part of Wolverton for 1000 years - except that it didn't have buildings on it.

Kim P. Well, that's what I mean Bryan is the housing estate development rather than the land itself. It's a bit hard to explain but as a small child I played on some of the estates as they were being built (back in the days when you could take your kids to work before health & safety freaked out about a small child trotting around a building site) so I tend to disassociate the land from the development. There's delineation in my mind between lands used for farming or that was undeveloped and new houses where people live.

Bryan D. I was just being pedantic, which I am prone to from time to time. Yes, "real" Wolverton was a community. The newer housing developments have become somewhat dissociated.

Pat B. When we were looking for a house in 1965 the Galleon Estate was on our list so we visited the site and we were not very impressed with the build at the time but it has stood the test of time and is now a very desirable place to live. Many Wolvey people moved over there.

Mark B. Lots of great and good memories of growing up on the galleon estate, from 1966 to 1989 when I moved away.

Joanna W. I lived on the Galleon Estate in Caxton road when the houses were still being built in Longville. Not aware of any local opposition but then again was only a wee girl of 9.

Ghosts

Soraya T. Apologies if this has been done before but. Let's have some Wooo-oooolverton ghost stories..?

Julie W. Zetters bingo hall quite haunted xx

Edward Q. Over Lucketts fields at top of Wolverton used to be a haunted house we used to go and visit

Julie W. Where's Lucketts fields? x

Edward Q. They used to be at the western end of Gloucester road prior to Woodland view etc being built Julie just all fields all the way round us.

Julie H. Think slated row opposite the church in Old Wolverton was supposed to be haunted

Phillip W. Stacey hill farm has a ghost of a girl.

Toni B. I'm not reading ANY of these. Watched a horror film last night had a nightmare. Lol

Soraya T. Bryan Dunleavy's gruesome train deaths article made me start this. Three deaths mentioned near the railway.... Makes you wonder..!

Julie W. They always said blue bridge was haunted xx

Soraya T. Our house in Cambridge Street was iffy. Definitely something going on in there although that might have been four very imaginative children (maybe).

Julie W. My house up Southern Way was bad.

Soraya T. What about St George's church... That always seemed very much NOT haunted. Much to my disappointment. I heard stories of the Gables, the two water towers, and the caretakers shed in Wyvern... Oh and the Horsa (?) hut at Bushfield!

Julie W. Oh yeah the caretakers shed in Wyvern definitely was I had to go in there and the nursery building xx

Barrie H. We use to sit round an old grave stone at night at St George's waiting for the witch to appear we'd got our chips and scratching with us though, this was quiet the thing back then no end of my school mates use to go, best time after a horror movie at the Empire.

Toni B. I always found Old Wolverton church creepy? Oh and the canal by the Galleon. At certain times a woman I believe?

Edward Q. Passenham is well noted for ghosts.

Kim P. When I was about 5 or 6 I used to tell my mum about a little old man who came into my bedroom at night and sat and watched me sleeping, I described a man in Edwardian type dress with a "sticky up" collar, balding with round wire framed glasses. My mum was a bit concerned at first but the more I talked about it the more she was convinced I was imagining it or dreaming rather than it being a real person. For whatever reason she happened to mention it to old Mrs. Essam who told her it sounded just like Mr. Dibb who had lived at our house at the turn of the century, she remembered him from when she was a child as a kind man who liked children and always had a smile or a sweet for them. I don't remember this bit but apparently Mrs. Essam dug up a picture of Mr. Dibb and showed it to me and I told her that was the man who came into my room at night. That was 47 Victoria Street. A few years after that my dad dug up a brass plated in the front garden that had his name on it and the date 8th March 1908. Charles Henry Dibb I think? Definitely Charles anyway.

Soraya T. Wow. That is a proper ghost story, thanks for sharing it!

Kim P. My mum also talked of two ladies she saw at 47 in the vicinity of the cellar door and stairs a couple of times, she didn't exactly hear them but more sensed them arguing, something to do with some plates which they both thought they were supposed to have inherited from someone and they were arguing about who was supposed to get them. She said they were sisters and thought their names were something like Sissie and Carrie. I never saw them though; I was scared of the cellar and didn't go round there any more than I had to loll

Toni B. KIM...I've just run cold. I'm not reading anymore. X

Julie W. I saw the ghost of a little the Zetters bingo hall when my mum worked there, was the first ghost experience I can remember x

Kim P. None of them were scary if that helps I'm not even 100% sure I believe in ghosts as such though I think they might be sort of images from the past that have hung around somehow, like an old movie that keeps playing or something.

Julie W. It's not scary at the time, it's only afterwards when u think about it and turn it in to more than it was xx

Toni B. It's strange how kids have many experiences. They say they're more receptive but lose it while growing?

Kim P. I think when you're a child you're more open minded aren't you, I mean if you believe in Santa Claus and dragons and the tooth fairy ghosts aren't too far behind. It's only when you get older and a bit more cynical and go "nigh that can't really be there" you lose it. My mum was always very open minded, her opinion was if you can see something it's probably there even if you don't know what it is, so I think that helped me to keep a sense of it into adulthood.

Jacqui H. I grew up in Jersey road, my parents are still there, and our house was occupied by the previous tenants who made themselves known every time we decorated!!! We heard them as children and sensed them!!! X

David M. Kim, I remember a Mr Dibb. He lived at the end house on Victoria Street where it meets Ratcliffe Street (or is it Stacey Avenue?). Our gang was always rather scared of him because he was liable to come out and shout at you! We called him Grumpus Dibb. Probably very unfair as we just used to try and annoy him!

Kim P. That's the house, David! When would that have been? When I was in France, among my stuff I found what looked to be an old microfiche printout of an obituary for Mr. Dibb from a local newspaper, I brought it back with me but of course now I want to look at it I can't find it anywhere.

Ian H. Is that the house the Woodward's moved to David?

Kim P. Woodward's rings a bell but I can't remember if my dad bought it from them or if they bought it from my Dad. We lived there 74-82 I believe.

Ian H. Woodward's lived there in the late 50's Kim

Geoffrey W. I can add a little to the conversation because, Kim was correct, in that we, the Woodward's, moved to 47 Victoria Street, or 48 Radcliffe Street as it was also called from having the shop on the square. Charles Dibb certainly did live there before us, and the story goes that he died there. He installed a system of bell pulls in each room so that he could call for assistance. I have no doubt that the house was haunted. Indeed, one evening I was sitting in the living room that could be by-passed by the hallway. Consequently it has 2 doors and as I was sitting there reading, I distinctly felt one door open, a rush of air as if someone was passing by behind me, then the other door open. I was terrified. My mother sold the house in approx. 1974, I think.

Pat G. When I moved into our house in Gloucester Road I often got the sense of being watched by a man. I had that sensation in the kitchen, and quite often in the bathroom when bathing the children. I thought nothing of it. Then one night one of the children woke me up. They were crying. I asked what was wrong. Where's the man gone? They asked. What man? The man who went to the wardrobe. Apparently this man had got out of the bed where my child was sleeping and walked over to the old built-in wardrobe and disappeared. The bed was one we had bought from the old lady who lived in the house before us. That really made me shivers! The next night I left a note with the new address of the previous owner. I said loudly that she wasn't in the house anymore and had moved to the address on the note. After that I had no more feelings of being watched etc. Could just have been coincidence I suppose but... Oh and I should add that we didn't have a television, so it wasn't something the children had seen on TV the night before.

Geoffrey W. Out of interest, what number Gloucester Road was that Pat?

Edith H. Yes Pat intrigued to know what number. I used to live at 31.

Pat G. Further up on the opposite side of the road. I think it was a Mrs Smith who owned it before us. A couple of doors away from the Fosters.

Edith H. Ah right yes so it must have been 54 my friend Pauline lived at 52

Pat G. No a bit further up still. As I don't live there any more I would rather not say because of the people who live there now. Don't want to put the eebie jeebies up them!

Peter L. You just reminded me Jacqui, some years ago I called on Tony Spensley, as I was leaving I looked up only to see Jo in the upstairs window with Kath standing behind him, later up the club I spoke to Jo and he insisted that Kath was not there, I said you are joking, now after reading your post I am wondering!

Jacqui H. That's right Pete; Mum had taken us out for the day we often talk about that x

Soraya T. I can remember only one spooky personal experience which happened to me. In our Cambridge street house I was in the sitting room and moving furniture. There was only me in the house and my mum in the garden. I left the room and when I came back in the furniture was a good foot away from the wall where I'd put it. I moved it back, left the room, came back, same again. I put it back, said 'stop it!' and it didn't happen again. Funnily enough at the time it wasn't spooky at all, just annoying. But the day my little sister came running down the stairs to say she'd just seen a man at the top of the stairs scared me

Barrie H. Any one heard of one-eyed Joe, the Bradwell Miller? He was killed crossing the Nobby Newport line. They do say every night when the moon is bright the Miller's ghost is seen. He walks the track with a sack on his back. He haunts the station. he haunts the mill, and the land that lies between

Janice M. My friend lived in Buckingham street 2 doors form the cemetery and they used to have weird things going on....and their dog used to sit and bark at the wall for no apparent reason, used to spook me out.

Len E. The house we live in was owned by a person who is deceased, and by all accounts was very proud of her home. My wife and children could always "sense" her presence and often talked about it. Then our cooker timer alarm started to go off on a regular basis always in the evening after the children had gone to bed. It got annoying having to turn the alarm off. Then it stopped happening. Only recently the girls told me that it was those coming downstairs and setting the timer for a few minutes then zipping back upstairs. Bloody kids!

Julie W. Quite a few of the southern way houses were odd, that's why I wondered what was on the ground before hand?

Chris G. Julie, did you know there's an Iron Age burial just a few yards from your old house, I didn't till quite recently.

Julie W. Is that true Chris or are you teasing me? x

Chris G. Nope totally true, just out the back.

Julie W. Where about is that situated?

Chris G. Roughly where they built that car park that was never used and is now overgrown on the other side of the 'forest'. I'll see if I can find the link to the website it's on later.

Julie W. OK I would like to see the proximity to my house. My friends mum saw the Bradwell Abbey Monks floating their way into the abbey in the 60's

Mike B. There's a bronze age ring ditch on the playing field of (what's now) Bushfield School at the top of Moon Street.

Maurice H. There used to be a spectre that appeared around one of the graves in the churchyard many years ago. It also appeared under the street light outside the drive to the old vicarage. It was white and moaned a lot. It turned out to be one of the older boys from school playing pranks. Although I was told that there was a ghost in the Churchyard really.

Mark B. My mates Paul Chapman from Windsor street and Dave Chambers from Oxford street, came haring back to my house in Longville saying they'd seen a monk near the church at Old Wolverton, I spent many years there, working and playing and never saw a thing. However a young lad playing on the mound next to the church (the Old Wolverton castle site) we felt someone was watching us and us all left quickly. No one was there, but it felt that we were being watched! Felt like that a few times since but never in Wolverton.

Elaine P. I used to live at number 3 Buckingham street, we knocked the dividing wall down between the two downstairs rooms, there was a 6ft long 'mound' under the floorboards.............we put the boards back rather I never did find out what it was.......... anyone care to go 'dig it up' !!!!!!!! Well, it WAS near the cemetery & could still be there!!!!

Bryan D. Fascinating anecdote Elaine. Your house was out in the fields beyond the churchyard at one time. I wonder if it was someone who was refused burial in the churchyard.

Brian E. Elaine, I would not have been able to resist having a poke around with a trowel.

Elaine P . OMG we was so scared, don't know HOW we lived there knowing that there was 'something' under the floor LOL I dare someone to go & see if it's still there!!!!!!!! he he

Julie W. I'll go and look, totally brilliant, was your house haunted x

Elaine P. Never had any 'experiences' Julie, but I would love to know if it was a body under there lol

Julie W. Wonder who lives there now x

Elaine P. This was 30 years ago now, so maybe someone has 'discovered' whatever it was by now lol

M1 Service Area Today

M1 Service Station

Barrie H. Did anyone else work here M1 service station (I worked here weekends and school holidays)

Jon H. Yes I did Dad loll

Steve B. Yes I did too.....evenings and weekends 1972/1973..... and I recall our horror when petrol went above 50p/gallon for the first time!

Barrie H. Who remembers Nosher Irani the manager there in the

112

late 60s?

Steve A. My mum worked there in the early days.

Brian E. I worked there on weekends. It was Blue Star garages then, managed by a man called Austin Long. I also remember Mr Irani at the cafe. I worked at Blue Star when we changed over to decimal currency, to the confusion of staff and drivers alike. Austin Long was an unpleasant fellow. He told me on one occasion he yearned for a return to mass-unemployment, so that he would not have to rely on long-haired hippy looking types like me to fill in at weekends. Does anyone remember when Myrtle Peach was a manageress there? What a remarkable woman she was. I know of few people who could swear as fluently as she.

Toni B. I worked there aged 14 sssssshhhhhh said I was 15 had a black nylon dress with white pinny and little hat.only lasted a few weeks no one famous came in-and that was all I wanted to see Stones, Monkees etc.lol
As Steve said our Mum worked nights in the 60s.

Len E. My elder brother worked there in the sixties and remembers a little known beat combo group come in....anybody heard of The Beatles?

Toni B. Nah....Len... stupid name any way.

Len E. Seemed to work for them Toni

Bryan D. I worked there as an assistant manager 1963-4. Fortes were probably the worst company I have ever worked for in my life! I even had to get a morning suit - black jacket and grey striped trousers. I had the suit made at the Co-op tailor on Church Street. It never fitted properly.

Brian E. Should have gone to Burton's Bryan!

Toni B. Wow Bryan... was your next job undertaker? lol

Bryan D. How dumb was I? I should've thought of that Toni, the I might have got my money's worth out of the suit - which I never wore again!

Steve B. I remember both Long and Peach.....what a double act they made! Both smoked like chimneys I recall.

Pat C. Used to call in there, early 60s very busy.

Gill B. My mum Ivy Robinson worked here from about 1958 until late seventies. When she worked the late shift I & friends would go up after the pub for a meal and get a lift back with her on Johnson's bus into Wolverton.

Barrie H. Johnsons use to drop us outside home in Southern Way.

John R. I did a stint - I cleaned tables in the Restaurant. I remember the manager Noshir Irani to this day - charming fellow.

Celia R. I worked there 1972 -1973 in the restaurant and on the pumps I remember Noshir Irani done my ankle in while I was working but I carried on to the end of the shift 11 o'clock at night.

Philip E. My wife worked there, Margaret Alderman in the early

60s.

Terry L. Dora Scott did!

Jennifer T. I worked there in 1961 in the restaurant, I got the United Counties bus from the western to the red house, the walked from there up the lane.

Chris G. Our Dad worked there early 60's on nights, not exactly sure of job title but had a smart uniform of long great coat and peaked cap, used to come home with autographs of all the stars, something else you wish you'd kept.

Jon H. I was there in 1990, they spotted my potential for greatness in the kitchens.... they made me an egg fryer. I did get quite good mind you!

Philip E. Margaret met the Beatles there in 1963 and got all there autographs was working in the restaurant at the time.

Angie A. My Gran worked there when I was a teenager.

Margaret C. My sister Alex Callow worked there for many years.

Brian E. I remember filling up Cliff Richards' yellow Lotus. Getting sworn at by Warren Mitchel lfor refusing to remove the radiator cap on his Jag. People said in real life he was nothing like Alf Garnett, but on that occasion he talked like him. Lulu & The Luvvers holding up the queue whilst they did autographs, and, most of all the continental truck-drivers who started turning up at around 4am, Newport being their first pull-in since leaving the ferry. They always had an abundance of duty-free cigarettes.

Glen B. When I was 16 worked there at "Julies Pantry" burger bar in 82...a bus used to pick us up from Cosgrove and take us to work had an excuse 3m plus unemployed back then I think

David E. I worked there in 75 for one month used to get picked up by mini bus from Southern way.

Mnemonics

Pina R. Can anyone remember any sayings or verses they were taught to remember things. The two I remember are - 'Richard of York gave battle in vain' - to remember the colours of the rainbow & in maths we were given the word 'bodmas' to remember the order in which to do our arithmetic - 'brackets over division, multiplication, addition & subtraction'......

Ron B. I before E except after C.

Andrew L. SOHCAHTOA

Colin T. Twiselton Get out of this class face the wall & put your hands on your head.......Me being a naughty boy......Again xxxx

Pat C. 30 days hath September, April June and November, all the rest have 31 except February which has 28 and 29 in each leap year.

Jean G. Never Eat Shredded Wheat, to learn where points of compass were.

Graham T. Some people have curly black hair through persistent brushing--Sine=perp over hypotenuse, cosine=base over hypotenuse;t angent=perp' over base.

Pat C. Remember remember the 5th of November, gunpowder treason and plot.

Maria M. I remember Sue Sawkins In Bushfield said this one. Big Elephants always use small exits. To remember how to write Because.

Penny G. Lazy fox jumps over the hedge" I think that was what it was as it supposed to be all the letters in the alphabet

Hazel S. The quick brown fox jumped over the lazy dog. That used all the letters on the keyboard.

Ian B. We used to run a test tape to test the comms/printers. "THE QUICK BROWN FOX JUMPS OVER THE LAZY DOG'S BACK 1234567890" the idea being it tested every character and upper and lower case.

Hazel S. Should have been 'The quick brown fox jumps over the lazy dog'. It has been a long while since I learnt this at Mrs. Holland's in the Wolverton Road, who gave shorthand and typing lessons.

Maurice W. TOACAHSOH

Pina R. Explain what they mean.

Maurice W. sorry, Tan=Opp/Adj, Cos=Adj/Hyp, Sin=Opp/Hyp

Andrew L. I was at a race meeting and I noticed the name of a racehorse was Sohcahtoa, and I couldn't work out why the name was familiar, so I thought about it for a minute and remembered the Bushfield trigonometry lessons. Oh, and Sohcahtoa was 25/1 so I backed him each way and he placed for a nice little payout. :)

Chris G. Was the jockey Douggie Sackett, Andrew? He loved that bloody word.

Moon St Pool

Jackie N. Talk of the swimming pool at Moon Street made me look out this photo- no date, so could use some help.

Bev P. As shallow as I remember it, you could "swim" with your hand on the bottom. The person watching has a jumper on so we all know how freezing the water is!!

Brian E. Amazing photo, thanks for posting. Rarely seen view. I would say, Summer mid-Sixties Jackie

Edith H. I remember that pool. I was at School until 64.

Andrew L. That wooden shack top right must have been demolished at some point that would help with the date. It was

Moon Street School Pool

certainly gone by 74 when I started there and the new block was already built then. Notice the chap standing in the water on the far right, and the other large chap standing in the water on the left of the pool both have Pedley haircuts.

Brian E. The old wooden shack was the woodwork room, then building ends you see are the Terrapin buildings, that one being Mrs. Woodward's needlework room...

Susan B. Didn't know Moon Street School once had a pool, I don't recall it there when I was there 69/70.

Andrew L. It was still there in '78, but by then it was surrounded by a wooden lap fence so you might not know it was there.

Hayley D. It was still there late 70's early 80's. Even though we did go to Watling way at Galley Hill quite a lot.

Wendy C. That was probably when it was good but when in my day at Bushfield hated it.

Sally C. Was there in the early 80's and was undercover - but still cold! Not there now, just a big mound and a conifer...

Jackie N. Was there until the 90s I think. In a previous post I mentioned that it was filled in -the cost of keeping it clean and adjusting the PH levels etc: plus vandalism -cracked tiles in the actual pool and damage to changing rooms-it just wasn't worth the hassle by then.........

Mick S. I remember this it was always so cold. I enjoyed swimming but never in this pool. The white floats on the side in the photo, we all used to learn to swim I can remember them clearly!

It was hidden behind a fence in my day, Mr Craddock used to teach us in there, but we also went to the proper pools in Wolverton, walking there and walking back, happy days.

Gareth G. Blimey that brings back memories. As well as the pool, the old dining hall in the background (cheese flan and apple crumble, mmmmm!) The old woodwork hut to the right (anyone remember the smell of that gluepot that was always heated up in lessons. What a stink.)

To the left of that, the old terrapin hut was my classroom in the 4th year class 4PB Mrs Woodward and was also the needlework room. I would say that the picture is a little later than my time so probably early 70s.

Janice M. I learnt to swim in that pool! Mr. Craddock in my opinion was an amazing teacher!

Brian E. Those are polystyrene floats you can see on the edge. It was strictly forbidden to throw these.

Steve W. Brian Craddock a legend of a teacher RIP

Debbie H. Mr Craddock was my teacher when he died...I cried for hours as I think he had a soft spot for me as he always stuck up for me as I was a naughty girl!! I remember the pool and the pottery room...where I had my first kiss at 12...on the steps...woo hoo. Obviously not with Mr Craddock....just to make that clear ha! - with a boy in my class.

Steve W. I remember him issuing us with rough books, and showing us an example of how he wanted us to write our names on the front. The example was Joe soap and Shane Kirk copied it word for word, so from that day Mr Craddock called him Joe Soap lol.

Terry L. Yes remember how bally cold it was, when you got out your skin felt like it was burning because you were so much warmer getting out. I thought the pool was nearer the fence to the backway! A good old pump there, looks set up to pump the water out rather than in!

Hayley M. It was definitely there when I was there between 1976-1980 and I did swim in it. The changing rooms were outside too... Blooming freezing and damn shallow! Yep, the building in the background had been replaced by a two storey building which housed the first and second years of Bushfield... Miss Georgeson was my teacher in there.

Andy M. I was at this school 1963 to 1967. Taught how to swim is this pool! The great Dan Crone was Headmaster and was instrumental in having this pool installed.

Brian E. And, Mr. Cockerill built the changing rooms.

Maria M. Was it really that open?

Dave P. Not when we were there Maria! - They had put a wall around it when we were there! Lol! and freezing damp changing rooms!!

Lisa P. Hideous memories of that pool. I much preferred the small pond just behind it. Not for swimming in (just in case you wondered) but for catching newts and toads. It was teaming with them. We weren't allowed to go there but that's what made it even more exciting. Anyone else remember the pond?

Dave P. Remember putting my right foot in it - bloody stunk all day!!!

Lisa P. Yeah, my friend Caroline Johnson and I got caught once and got a good telling off but the teacher, who hadn't even known the pond was there, suddenly became quite interested in it and we ended up bringing a toad into the classroom in a jam jar for everyone to draw. A nice memory.

Ian S. I nearly drowned in that pool after falling in as a youngster while my mum played tennis at some courts nearby my brother pulled me out in the nick of time.

Dave P. They have dye in pools now to catch those kids at it!! I lost count of how many 'warm' patches I must have swam through in that pool!! Urgh.

Chris G. Used to be tennis courts out the back of Ken Speaks house just near there, are they still there anyone?

Vince C. Gill will know about courts. Used to play the odd set with Gary.

Janet B. No Chris. I visit Vera Ken's widow and I do believe the land was sold they had quite a chunk of it.Gill Beales would know more about this as she lives a few doors down.

Chris G. I know the old entrance now has a garage over it so suspected as much.

Gill B. Yes you are right, Ken & Vera bought the land and he used to keep his chickens there. We did have some good times when it was a tennis club. It was so handy at the bottom of our gardens & very safe for the children.

Prom

Brian E. Wearing my grumpy old man hat, I get really annoyed when I hear modern school kids refer to their 'prom.' This is annoying enough in American school (I have taught in an American school). I bet most of them, if asked would have no idea what 'prom' actually means. Parts of modern youth culture refer to the police as 'the Feds.' This they can only have got from American films. Trick or treat is bad enough.

Julia B. Didn't care what it was called, what I did care about was the huge amount of cash that was wasted on it!

Brian E. There is a taxi firm in MK that advertises stretched limos for "proms!"

Julia B. Exactly! why why!

Brian E. Because that's what they do in America! All those sub-rate High school Movies have an effect!

Jane B. Blimey - in my day we didn't even get an "End of Year Disco" - but thinking back - hmm, maybe just as well !!!!

Bev P. My daughter looked like a Princess for her American High School Prom. Saying that I would probably hate it creeping into UK schools if I still lived there. Living here it wasn't annoying and she and most of her friends worked very hard to help pay for everything.

Bryan D. Prom in the US; Grad in Canada - but essentially the same ceremony to mark the end of High School. There is no equivalent way to finish school in the UK, so what are these fake proms in the UK all about?

Brian E. Bryan, I hear it everywhere. At the school at which I taught some of the American teachers even organised Grad. parties at the end of 7th or 8th grades!

Chris G. And its not just the end of secondary school here, leaving middle school for the comp they have one at eleven now too. Bloody American imports! Just don't get me started on those who have started putting their hand over their heart singing the national anthem. Grrrrrrrrr (old, grumpy and loving it!)

Pat C. Over here Debs Balls for the last 30ish years when leaving secondary

Bryan D. I was wondering why we weren't influenced by film in the same way - but on reflection, I suppose we were. Teenagers had just been invented and because they had purchasing power (in the US at any rate) there was a spate of films in the early 50s about disaffected youth: Blackboard Jungle, The Wild Ones, Rebel without a Cause. However they didn't make films about Prom Night or scary witchy-poo Halloween, so we carried on with our own traditions. And by the way we went to see a film or to the flicks - "movies" were not part of the language.

John Rd. I think you lot are just old and cant keep up with the times. Hell I bet your parents said the same kind of things about your youth and how the times had changed ;)

Bryan D. I'll speak for myself John. I am old and there are some things I am not interested in keeping up with. I have found it relatively easy to adapt to modern technology, for example, but I frankly can't be bothered with films that are targeted at 12 year olds or wannabe out-of-key singers on talent shows. I've got plenty to amuse me thanks. And I reserve the right to be a grumpy old man if I choose. For one thing, I've earned it and for another, nobody is going to pay attention to me anyway. So I may just as well enjoy spouting off!

Chris G. You'll be the same before you know it John, complaining about kids with holograms for friends and telepathic phones and us all swearing allegiance to the stars n stripes... ;)

John Rd. Yeah, no doubt I will but I've got a few years yet before that happens, my son is only 8 months old ;) As for swearing allegiance to stars an stripes...well if I caught my boy doing that then he going to get a slap! English an proud

Brian E. That's the point, John. I am not complaining about 'young people today,' it is the massive American influences. An end of year or term dance/disco/bash/party is fine. It is hearing it called the Prom annoys me.

Brian E. How long before we hear people here saying 'do the math!'

John Rd. It was called a prom(that was before high school musical an the likes) even when I left school, though I never went, wasn't my scene. As for yank influences well what goes around comes around after all we influenced them during the industrial revolution and now they just returning the favour.

Donna S. I hear you Brian... live in Canada where they have grade 8 grad and then again after high school..... as a student and a parent who has been involved in education system over here I shudder to think these young people are our future..... oh they know computers and they know how to text ask them a basic math question or how to spell a word and they look at you like you from a different planet. Ask them what 2 x 6 is or how to count change unless a calculator is used or a machine to tell them they haven't got a clue . sure there are a few rare smart ones but all in all its pretty sad. .. as for American influence well I have long said just a matter of time before Canada becomes the 53rd state....but then again there is enough blame to go around ... from parents to teachers to school boards to govt.... not enough funding etc... teachers who in general well I wont go so far as to say they don't care but long gone are the days when teachers would stay behind after school to help a student(with very few exceptions) my daughter going through it now with her daughter.. she helping her do her homework etc says to me mum I went to school why do I have homework just way it is parents are encouraged to be more involved due to the aforementioned shortages .

Bryan D. And on the subject of Americanisms creeping into language over here (which I don't mind if it has some meaning to the people who use it and hear it) but I frequently hear "stepping up to the plate" used over here on radio and TV. Now I know what it means because I have watched baseball and played softball, but I seriously doubt if 90% of the UK audience have any idea what it means or where it came from.

Jane B. Well I certainly don't Bryan - thought it was something to do with eating!!! Learn something new every day - oh, and the phrase I hate is "Have a good day" !!!!

Bev P. Many years ago my son (now 27) "graduated" from elementary school. They had them march into the room and played the music they play at all graduations here" Pomp and Circumstance". Now to me that is Land of Hope and Glory. For some reason being so far from home it just hit me and I started crying, not the done thing for the English, but everyone around me thought I was just overcome with emotion about my son!! I have managed to control myself at all other graduations since. :)

Brian E. Bryan, I suppose the nearest English equivalent is 'toe the line.' From the early days of boxing.

Bryan D. Possibly, "making a stand at the crease" might be closer, from the game with similar origins. "Stepping up to the plate" is usually applied to describe critical situations in the game where a key hit or home run is required to rescue the game. It is a high pressure situation and therefore the metaphor is used in real life, often crisis situations where some leadership is required. I can't imagine an American broadcaster saying "President Obama's on a sticky wicket."

Sellicks Garage

Len E. Didn't Sellick have a garage on 27 Church St in Wolverton? As I recall it had a shop front with petrol pump outside on the pavement and at the back was a garage/workshop my dad worked for Sellicks and that is where we lived in early 60's

Jill G. It had changed a bit by the time I moved to Bradwell in 1965 I remember it had a couple of lovely old cars in the shop front.

Vince C. Where was that in relation to now?

Chris G. I remember that old garage in Church St Len, even when the building was derelict that pump still stood out front. I'm sure there's a pic somewhere on here with it.

Ron B. Just past the Dance studio heading towards Newport Think there are houses on this site now. Just before turning up to Old Bradwell.

Vince C. Did the Church Street site become Russ Jones' yard before the houses were built? There used to be an old pump there.

Chris G. Nope it was down the other end Vince, where Russ's place was used to be the council yard.It would be roughly where the bus stops are now.

Len E. I've looked Chris can't seem to find one; my dad took some photos of Church St before they pulled the buildings down.

Shame I can't find them :(

Chris G. Yes I've searched 'Church street Wolverton' in Google images and although you can see the building a couple of times, you can't quite make out the pump for definite.

Sellicks Garage on the Stratford Road

Colin T. There's the little office I was talking about Nice one Vince, thanks for these picture's they bring back fantastic time's when I was helping me Dad out at work,

Ron B. Under the name of WG Sellick's Pre decimalisation. Victor FB under canopy

Jackie N. I remember the garage being Sellick's my dad did the electrics for it-he was friendly with Mr Sellick think he did the work with Pete Coleman

Brian E. How many coaches did Sellick's have, does anyone know?

Ron B. Not that many Brian. My dad used to drive for them. I remember they were Bedford OB coaches in the fifties

Terry L. Brother in law reckons 1968; Munro Moore took over in 70/71 and changed it to Wolverton Motor Co....

Ruth E. Think my ex father in law Frank Berry either worked at Sellick's or drove buses, also I believe Johnny Johnson worked there at some point,

Terry L. Great Pic's thanks for sharing, guessing it would be late 60's early 70's.I will ask my Bro in law who did his apprenticeship there, he will narrow the date down for us! Pre decimalisation anyway.

Vince C. It remained a Burmah garage until it closed I believe. I worked there part time weekends on the Petrol and on the hire fleet then for a few weeks after I left college until Aug 1988.

Ron B. Great pic Vince. Victor 101 estate Mark 2 Jag Moggie minor and Victor fb on forecourt. Watch this space for corrections and amendments.

Vince C. I remember on my first day on the hire fleet I reversed a Transit with a tail-lift into another hire car. I had to phone up the MD (Munroe Moore) and ruin his Sunday breakfast. He was surprisingly good about it. Does anyone remember the name of Wolverton Motor Co chain smoking Accountant? Was it Ron? Other names I remember were Steve Barry, Tony Dolly, Mark Pyner, and Ian Barry. Anyone remember any of the Car Salesmen names around the eighties?

Colin T. Morning Vince, Fantastic picture, Good times, My Dad (Bless Him) use to serve Petrol & I use to hand out the Green Shield Stamps

Morning Ron, You ok xx, Do you remember The little wooded Box in the middle of the petrol pumps It had a sliding door & inside we had a little shelf with the Till on it & a chair to sit on LOL, You imagine todays work force putting up with those conditions xx

Pat C. Snr Very good Ron, what's the sideways on one? Is that a Triumph rear end?

Vince C. . In my day we sat in a little area at the front of the building and used to keep the sliding door unlocked until a spate of holdups in Bucks so we had to lock it and use the little hatch. If you did the late shift you were on your own for a few hours after Hire closed up. Was quite a responsibility at 17?

Ron B. Yes I remember that well Colin. Pat, think it looks like a Triumph 2000tc?

Vince, didn't a guy called Ray Lawrence work on the sales side?

Vince C. Rings a bell. There was an older guy and two (?) Younger guys as I recall. I think the accountant may have been called Pat actually??

Ron B. I think there is a pic on the Bradwell site of Sellicks garage in Newport road. Will post on here.

Jane B. When I was there the Accountant was a bloke called Mick (he chain smoked) - but can't recall his surname. This would be late 1983/early 1984 - Les Hubbard ran the Spares Dept. and his wife Molly worked in the office - along with Ron's wife (but can't remember her name either)!!!!!! Les Lee on Hire Desk along with John Dewick, Steve Barry and Nigel the South African lad!!!! Sales were Michael Shaw and Tom Main - think these names are right - someone will correct me if not!!!!!!

Vince C. Jane, I couldn't remember the accountant, thanks for that. I remember two Johns on hire. Was John the taller faired haired one in charge? Many years ago I saw him again; he was working at the John Lewis Warehouse at Granby. I think there was another salesman called Richard in my day (87-88).

Jane B. John Dewick was tall and blonde - and yes, I believe he later worked at John Lewis. He is now about 56/7 as he was at school with my hubby. Can't remember the Accountant's surname - but it's on the tip of my tongue so it'll come to me later!!! All I remember is that he had longish hair and wore a brown suit - oh, and he came from Stony Stratford.

Ron B. I fit that bill Jane. Wasn't me though.

Julian W. I remember going there as a Scout on bob-a-job week. They got us to tidy-up the workshop. We then spent what seemed like an hour getting clean with Swarfega.

Terry L. John Dewick still at JLP last I heard!

Chris. G Terry am I right thinking Evil Hank either worked or helped out here?

Terry L. Don't remember that mate, but a good possibility as his Dad bought his cars from there and I suppose Munroe Moore was a drinking buddy of the good Doctor...

Jane B. Munroe and Doc Hall were best pals - think EH worked on the pumps for a while in his teenage years. By the way Vince Clinton - think the Accountant was Mick Hillier (or a very similar surname)!!!!

Vince C. I remember when they gutted the bungalow to become W M Company's offices.

Karen T. I have memories of Wolverton Motor Company for a different reason. The company sponsored the Radcliffe Rollers Steel Band that I played in from 1985. I remember great parties at Munroe Moore's house and we'd perform at them. We had a Wolverton Motor Co lorry for transporting the steel pans too. We performed once in the actual garage briefly. That was when we won the first heat for the Saturday Superstore Search for a Superstar competition and we had the local press down there taking photos. Got some myself that day too, will try and find them and post them. Very very happy days, the steel band was everything to me during school so good on you Munroe Moore for helping us!

Julia B. Bless, think Mark Bennett worked there on a Sunday... May be wrong.

Mark Bn. Yep, I worked there on the pumps on Sundays in the late 70s and early 80s. I worked on the pumps with Trevor 'squib' Squires I remember Jon Dewick on rentals, old Taftie was a mechanic. Monroe Moore the boss. It was Tony Dolling son of Sid] and Tom Main in sales. I also worked there in school hols and the mechanics sent me to the stores for a long weight and a bucket of steam [how naive we were in those days]

Richie B. The furthest white cars a Ford Zephyr or Zodiac.

Billy L. The days when Wolverton was a real community.

Short Back and Sides

Karen W. Here's a picture of my Grandad inside the shop.

George Pedley Hairdresser

Edward Q. Your Grandad cut my hair many many times Karen.
Jane B. My Dad used to go there in the late 60's to have his hair cut - I used to be allowed to sit in the vacant chair on the children's seat - thought I was so grown up!!!!!!!
Richard R. Had my hair cut there many times as a youngster,

George was a top bloke!

Ron B. Crikey. That's brought back some memories. Shame it can't do the same for my hair.

John R. Didn't he also have a helper, I think it was Vic, I remember going there with my dad.

Chris G. Take a look in the background John. Great pic Karen.

Chris G. Here you are Christian Bowler Vic in the reflection.

Christian B. Aw that's Brilliant I used to love my uncle (great) Vic. He still used to cut hair for the old boys round Wolverton, always used to cycle everywhere, great picture thank you x

Ian S. Eek that the fella that used to cut my hair (when I had some) it always had that smell of Brylcream in the shop.

Doug M. Oh my goodness that picture took me right back. My dad took me in there to get my hair cut. Peddlys right. Had a picture of a Sergeant Major saying < am I hurting you son, I should be I am standing on your hair.

Len E. So smartly dressed.

Terry L. Many visits to George Pedley and Vic as a kid, happy times and hair !

Steve W. Vic cut my ear once, long time since I have been to the barbers.

Terry L. It must have been the stuff coming out of the works chimney that made us all bald; we should consider suing them Steve!

Steve P. That's why I got my own clippers & have never paid for a haircut for over 30 years. When the boys were young had an option of no 1, 2, 3, or 4. Surprisingly enough the girls never took up the option.

Brian E. The Asian barber on Stratford Road next to the Western still only charges £5. And he does eye-brows, ears & nose as a matter of course. Wolverton must have more barbers per capita now than any other similar town?

Jon H. Every 4 weeks without fail my Grandad would take me in there for for hair cut, he would say short back and sides Vic, and so would I. I remember he had a booster seat for me to sit on.

Brian E. Back then, short back 'n' sides were the only haircut on offer!

Ron B. And something for the weekend sir? lol

June L. Pete always went to Mr Cummings in Cambridge St for his hair cut it cost him Half-a-Crown, then when he stopped cutting hair he got me to do it & I've been cutting his hair ever since, I don't touch the top though. P.S, nothing for the weekend.

Ron B. Ah Sid Cummings. Went there a few times

Chris G. When we were about ten (72ish) a group of us went in to get skinheads like the big boys, varying degrees of success depending if George or Vic cut it, I'm sure Steve Watts and

Graham Smith remember it well. Bargain at 20p though!

Christian B. George looked like he had massive hands, could be the camera angle though.

Dave B. Well those hands gave me a few short back 'n sides as a kid.

Trimmers

Maurice H. Does anyone know if there was any truth in the old story that when a Coach came into the works, and the Seats were taken into the shops, that the guys used to line up along the benches with mallets or hammers and when the seat was cut open they use to splat the fleas that came out?

Steve A. Quite possible, I was a trimmer in the works when they were still using horse hair and the stuff that came out of them was filthy! There was a separate shop that just dealt with the 'stripping out' the horse hair then went through a carding...

Mike W. My favourite works story, old cos Granddad told it to me, a bloke was gathering scrap timber, putting it in a barrow, getting the timber approved for removal, and off he went, out of the main gate. Did this loads of times before anyone worked out he was nicking the barrows.

Chris G. The mallets and hammers were to fight each other off for the loose change that fell out those seats.

Pete B. I brought one of those barrows 10 years ago. It is now rotting under my orchard, has proper leaf springs and axle. Free to good home !

Mike W. Though the story was probably true, he was nicking the barrows and flogging them then!! Granddad (Fred Wright) worked as a carpenter so would have done stuff on the royal train as well as most of the rolling stock at the time. His pic I believe is in one of the train makers book series, can't remember which page he is on though.

Phillip W. Pete, I know the arts and heritage group would like to have it it's going for free.

Wolverton Boundaries

Gary K. Following on from the post regarding Wallace St, I wanted to add that lots of weird and wonderful boundaries existed in the 19th century. When tracing Stony Stratford (Bucks) members of my family tree, I soon discovered that the town came under the registration district of Potterspury (Northants). I believe the same was true for Wolverton.

In 1927 the Potterspury district was abolished, but from 1837 until that time our Wolvertonian relatives would have been registered as being born in Northamptonshire.

Chris G. Agreed it can throw you. I did some research for someone from Stony recently and the Northants reference had me totally off the trail for a while.

Bryan D. An Act of 1832 created what were known as Poor Law Unions. The idea was to take the burden of looking after the poor from the individual parish and allow freer movement. For example, if you wanted to move from Wolverton to Stony Stratford you would need a guarantor to ensure you didn't become a cost to the local ratepayers. This set up the Potterspury district which, as you say, lasted until 1927. It did not change county boundaries. If you were born in Stony you were born in Bucks; if you were born in Old Stratford you were born in Northants. Every birth, marriage and death was registered in the Potterspury district.

Gary K. I agree Chris. I remember a hilarious bit of badinage years ago when my grandmother wanted to apply for a passport and had to dig our her birth certificate. She insisted she was born in Stony and refused to take the application form to the post office with "Potterspury" written in as the place of birth!

Bryan D. That seems to be an annoying quirk on the Ancestry site Chris. Some transcribers who doesn't know geography has automatically assumed that Wolverton is in Northants because of the Potterspury thing. It's only on 1901 I think.

Gary K. Thank-you Bryan - I knew you'd know! So did the 1832 Act have something to do with the formation of the Workhouses too, then, assuming from what you say that individual parishes no longer had to provide alms for the poor?

Bryan D. Yes Gary and the workhouse was in Potterspury. Maybe still there.

After the reorganisation the new district for us Wolverton types was Newport Pagnell.

Gary K. Not much improvement there, then!

My birth certificate says registration district as North Bucks, sub-district Newport Pagnell, so they'd definitely sorted us all out into the correct county by then!

Penny G. I was born in New Bradwell & the registration district was Newport Pagnell I was born 1948.

Stephen C. Potterspury district must have been abolished later than 1927. My Father was born in Wolverton in 1929 and his birth certificate was Potterspury. Same with my Mother who was born in Stony in 1933.

Bryan D. You're right Steve, the posted dates were too early. The local Government Act of 1930 abolished the Poor Law Unions and their responsibilities were taken over by Local and County Councils. There may have been a period of overlap while offices sorted themselves out.

Stephen C. Just googled it Bryan. Abolished 1935.

Kevin S. An ancestor of mine resided in the Potterspury Workhouse......many a harrowing tale could be told about them I'm sure. There were 3 in Newport I understand including the old Renny Lodge building.

The Wolverton Express

The Wolverton Express announces the new city in 1964

Harvey A. Discussion on newspaper rounds elsewhere brought up the Wolverton Express so I thought it appropriate to start a new thread. The proprietor of the Express and of the shop that was part of it, was A J (Alf) Emertpn until the end of 1949. When he retired A E (Bert) Foxford became Editor-in-Chief and my father's elder brother Len (Joe) became chief reporter and Advertising Manager. They were the owners of the business. In January 1950 dad left his job at the Works and became Manager of the Shop, joining Peggy Lovesey who was already there. Those were the days when reporters went out to all sorts of humdrum events to gather news (and in the process of course built up a network of news contacts which became important sources of information over the years). I remember even when we lived at Haversham, getting on my bike and going with Uncle Len to flower shows at Hanslope and other places and even better going with him on the team bus to away matches he was reporting on Wolverton FC. We moved to Wolverton in about March 1952 (or 53) when mum and dad bought the house next to the shop (101) when Alf and Kitty Emerton moved to Tring. I then remember going to Bedford on Thursday morning in school holidays when Uncle Len went with the final copy for that week's issue of the Wolverton Express to be printed at the presses of the Bedfordshire Times in Bedford. I have no idea how copy and advertising got there otherwise, or what happened in the days before cars were so common. But it was fascinating to see the process at work, from the setting up of type to the create of hot metal and the running of the presses. Later, in the afternoon, we would bring back our own shop copies which we then had to fold and markup for delivery next day. My recollection is that about 200 copies were sent by mail to subscribers from across the country and even to other places across the world. After ten years mum and dad decided that they wanted to own their own business so the family moved away (I had already left the nest by then) and bought a shop in Somerset. **David M.** Fascinating ! Really miss the "Buster" as Dad always

Wolverton Express Staff

From left: Beryl Wilson, Pamela Lockett, Peggy Lovesey, Molly Worth, Ann Lovesey, Nancy Allen

called it for some reason. Spent half an hour only yesterday in MK library looking up some of the editions from the seventies for family related articles. It really does make fascinating reading **Jackie N.** I lived in Oxford Street in the 1950s, when the Foxfords lived at no.24. I was friendly with Sandra. Years later I came back to Oxford Street and ended up living at -no. 24!

Martin G. I was at school with Joanne, the Foxfords lived in Frankston Ave.Stony in the late 60's

Harvey A. Thank you Jackie, I've been trying to remember where the Foxfords lived and you are right of course. It was Oxford Street, in the 50s anyway. Bert was a very nice guy, and the core around which the paper evolved week by week. Yet he had a very cute sense of humour and I remember my mum saying that if he was in a party he could often be persuaded to recite 'There's a one eyed yellow idol to the north of Katmandu', which he knew in its entirety. There were occasionally disparaging remarks about the Buster, as there would be for any semi-successful enterprise, but I think its strength lay in that they were good old-fashioned reporters prepared to go to fetes and funerals, meetings and socials, courts and sports, in order to know their territory and build a network of contacts. **Colin Griffiths** I used to have the Express sent to me in Australia in the 60's and early 70's and remember one Monday morning getting the previous Friday paper! It was supposed to be sent by surface mail. I have an odd edition stored away in the garage and some clippings. What was the date of the last edition?

Elizabeth M. Don't forget the weddings that used to go in the paper, with a list of bridesmaids, etc and some of the guests. Used to love reading it. Still have to cuttings from my wedding and my sisters wedding.

Bryan D. Pamela Lockett cut her reporting teeth there in 1958. I'm sure she has a lot of memories. Headline news was usually some council debate about rate increases or yet another decision NOT to build the swimming pool. Harry Saunders and Spencer Tapp were frequently recorded at the Magistrate's Court for some affray or other, and Pat Hayden of 119 Gloucester Road was a regular writer of letters to the editor. I think his son was a near contemporary of yours Harvey.

Pamela L. Happy days. Bert Foxford was living in Stony Stratford when I started on the Express and died very suddenly after a short illness. What a gentleman! Taught me so much. He was highly regarded by Lord Campbell who was the head of the newly formed Milton Keynes Development Corporation. I actually started work as a junior reporter with the Bucks Standard at Newport Pagnell and then moved on to the North Bucks office of the Chronicle and Echo, then based in Church Street. One of my jobs was to ensure the late racing results were printed in the column on the right of the paper. the actual printing was done by someone called Yvonne Richardson who lived in Windsor Street. Also working on the Chron at the time was Richard Pointer who lived in Windsor Street. We worked together on the Express in later years and also in Northampton on the Northants Post. I moved on to edit papers in Bedfordshire, Northamptonshire and Oxfordshire and Richard eventually ended up at the Daily Mail as did his wife Chris who he met while working at the Express. I also used to go to Bedford to see the papers printed but an earlier memory is when I worked on the Bucks Standard which had its own printing press and on a Thursday night we used to handfold the paper while eating fish and chips.

I well remember Pat Hayden. What a firebrand! And the council meetings in the offices on the Market Square at Stony, now Taylors estate agents, with Donald Morgan and Aileen Button staunch labour supporters. And the council clerk I think his name was Harboard or something similar a very straight laced character. He was a Quaker I believe like Mr Morgan if not some other fringe religion.

The Lovesey girls what a beautiful group of sisters who could dance like a dream their Dad Joe was a band leader I think.

Bryan D. Sorry Pamela, I probably wasn't paying attention. I thought you went straight to the Express.

Pamela L. No problems; great to remember.

Colin G. Aileen Button I believe was a teacher at the Grammar School. I have hazy memories of the Lovesey girls, Pat is a name I remember, is this one?

Harvey A. Pamela, I've seen your name on here and I felt I knew it from somewhere. I had started working in London by the time you started at the Express Office so didn't see much of you. Molly Hudson had been working there for three or four years by that time - I think she moved to Cheddar in Somerset when she got married in the 1960s. Somewhere I've got a photo with you all on taken at about the time mum and dad left at the end of 1959. I will try to find it.

Pamela L. I can remember that photo but it is in the UK at my old house where my daughter lives. Molly married Eric Worth from Old Stratford and they had three children. We went to visit them in Cheddar and had a great time on scrumpy. Also at the Express at that time were Gerald Stratton who still lives in Newport Pagnell, Roy Pateman from New Bradwell who died very young and his wife Beryl Wilson from Stacey Avenue who I think also died young. Those were the days before MK when the staff was quite small. I knew your uncle as Joey a school pal of my dad Jack Bellamy. My great uncle Bill Stephenson also used to work at the Express and moved on to become circulation manager of the Manchester Guardian. It must be from him I got my idea of becoming a journalist an ambition I had as long as I can remember. My son Jon Lockett followed in my steps and until he took redundancy last Christmas was associate editor of the Daily Star. His wife was news editor of the Press Association. The Express archives were sent to Stacey Hill museum when the Express closed I do not know if they are still there. Coincidentally when we moved to Spain 13 years ago and started lawn bowls, golf being too expensive, the first person I bumped into was Geoff Farrington from Wavendon who used to be in my class at Wolverton Grammar until they split off to become Bletchley Grammar and was a junior reporter on the Bletchley Gazette the same time I was at the Bucks Standard. Small world! I had not seen him for 45 years.

Ruth E. My wedding picture along with a full description was in The Express,they also used to print all the mourners names at funerals....I still have my cutting...

Pamela L. Hi Ruth that was one of my first jobs standing outside the church door collecting names for the funerals and pity you if you asked some VIP, in his or her opinion, for their name and he or she were most offended giving you an icy stare walking off and leaving you terrified until some kind soul supplied their name.

Harvey A. I can quite understand the continuing allure of news and reporting, Pamela, and pleased that it has continued in your family. You must feel proud at your son's achievement. Back in about 1957, one time we all went up to Fleet Street to see the Daily Express being 'put to bed'. I can still imagine the smell of newsprint that pervaded that place (as also it did the Beds Times building). Being still at school I didn't contribute to the paper except for the occasional item on sport at school, but even now in retirement I find myself contributing regularly to our Village magazine and to our Chapel newsletter, and enjoying the creative process. When mum and dad retired in early 1975, and my wife and I left London to join my brother in running their shop, it was the news, magazine and book section that I saw as my special responsibility among the other things I did. Of the staff at the Express Office, I knew Gerald Stratton though he was part time then, I think, looking after news in the Newport area. I assume that he became full time when Uncle Len (Joe) retired.

Harvey A. Somewhere back up there Bryan is a reference you made to Pat Hayden's son. As you know, in those days we had two stabs at passing the scholarship, and in that lottery, I passed first go and arrived at WGS soon after my tenth birthday. I then 'caught up' by having two years in the third form (I really don't know whether going to WGS early was a good idea or not), so in that way I embraced two years of students. I think I can remember a Hayden from the earlier year but don't remember a first name. Living in Haversham when we started there I was put in Green House and stayed there even after we moved to Wolverton. In the tribal atmosphere of Houses, and that he would have been a year up on me in the senior part of the school, there's an explanation why I have no recollection of him at this moment. As for your comment Colin, yes Aileen Button taught English and was our teacher for English at A level (and very good too I think).

Bryan D. I don't recall his first name either. I think his nickname was "Plug" or something like that. I did know his younger sister Bridget at one point in my life.

Ruth E. And what a small world Pam! My daughter Sarah 'Berry' Smith & her husband Terry Smith know your son Jon very well, xx

Kim P. Not a memory of newspaper round but of the newspapers themselves. When I was in my mid teens I was involved with the Wolverton drama group, my parents had an antiques collection they opened occasionally for charity and also I ran a local branch of (of all unlikely things) the national Goon Show Preservation Society. This was in the 1980's. I remember going and sitting in the Citizen office at the junction of Church & Radcliffe Streets sometimes for two hours telling them, "Hey we have something REALLY exciting going on if you want to come and talk to me!" and almost always eventually someone came and talked to me and we got a bit in the local paper about our latest play or show or event. they were really good about printing local stuff even if they didn't think it was that earth shattering.

Carol P. Hi Pamela. I remember your name well from those days. Richard and Chris are still happily married and now live in Oxfordshire. They recently met up with Gordon Rogers, who I believe worked there, or the Chronicle & Echo. The photographer was a John Barrett or something. xx

Pamela L. Hi Carol great to hear about Chris and Richard didn't realise they lived in Oxfordshire. Richard worked on the Chron as did Gordon. John Barrett the photographer unfortunately died several years ago. For many years after the Express closed we used to meet annually on the day the paper shut but sadly, as we grew older, some died and others like myself moved abroad, but please give my best wishes to Chris and Richard when you are next in contact.

Carol P. I will do Pamela xx

Colin G. Hi Pamela. When did the Express close?

Pamela L. I will find the exact date for you but from memory I think 33 years ago.

Wolverton in 1912

Phillip W. Thinking a lot about Titanic and 1912 I wonder what living in Wolverton in 1912 would have like you think no internet or mobiles in fact do u think we could have lived in that time.

Jill G. Life would have been hard but simple I suppose

Phillip W. I think it would have been better in some ways than today

Terry L. A Titanic Survivor lived in Wolverton Phillip , Ronnie Humphries Gran ???

Chris G. Strange to think that in another 100 years our ancestors will probably look back on us in 2012 thinking what a hard life we led.

Phillip W. I know I always wonder what live would have been like if I lived in 1912 I think I would like to stay in 2012 though.

Pat C. Chris will it be ancestors or robots in a 100 yrs?

Pat C. Re Titanic interesting and sad article in Mirror today about how Titanic affected one town and certain streets.

Phillip W. I hear they want to try and rise the ship

Pina R. Don't have to go back to 1912 to wonder what it would be like without internet or mobiles......we didn't have them when we were growing up....

Donna S. Exactly Pina... we didn't have them then.. more to the point what would we have done without electric or gas.... could we have survived without that .. I think so.... as with anything you learn to adapt in order to survive..

Len E. Phillip, doubtful if they could do that as it broke in two, also it is a dedicated grave yard for those that went down with it although there would be no visible human remains. Since they found the wreck they have brought artefacts up.

Phillip W. I feel it should stay in its resting place

Richie B. They won't raise the titanic as Len said its protected they say in another 50 years it will be a pile of rust its collapsing now.

Julie W. Being a major sad Titanic buff, I'm loving the 100th year anniversary.

Richie B. Me too the series is on tonight

Phillip W. I find it so interesting how there is so much of the ship still there I love seeing the inside of the ship as it is today

Julie W. I don't believe any of the conspiracy theories, it was in the wrong place at the wrong time xx

Phillip W. They reckon that the ship on bottom of the sea is the Olympic but I believe it is titanic

Chris G. Went to the exhibition at Greenwich a few years ago when some artefacts were first put on show, as you left there was a huge spanner set in the wall that you could touch, quite spooky knowing the history and all that.

P .Webb I have never seen any thing from titanic in real life just in books and on TV

Julie W. I went to Southampton a few years and met Malvina Dean the last living survivor, but sadly she died recently xx

Phillip W. Is a dream of mine to one go down to the wreck

Len E. I can understand people wanting to salvage parts of the ship, but to me it is grave robbing

D.Scott Yes... some things best left alone... leave her where she rests....

Julie W. I'd love to go to Nova Scotia and see the cemetery, xx

Chris G. We've got a loose family connection to it, EJ Smith the future captain of the Titanic, learnt his trade serving under a relation of ours Capt Benjamin Gleadell, skipper of the SS Celtic, also a White Star ship, doing transatlantic crossings in the 1880s.

Richie B. They bought up one of the metal panels that was stamped with the Titanic's id number I think but not sure it was 308 but it proved it was the Titanic and not its sister ship.

Julie W. It was Titanic, people like a drama xx.

Xmas

Len E. As we approach Christmas some of you might be looking forward to your children's/grand children's school nativity play. Were any of you a Joseph or a Mary? Or like me....a Tree!!! Standing on the stage at the age of 6 waving my arms in the air going woo woo has left me emotionally scarred. I know my acting skills are wooden. But really!

Jane B. In the first year of the Junior School I took the lead in our Christmas play - named "The Broken Plate" - yep, you've guessed it - I WAS THE PLATE !!!!!! Spent the whole of the play on stage sitting on a chair with a big cardboard plate tied to my front - remember Gaynor Lee was the Chimney Pot - and David Wallace was a soldier - apart from that I think I've erased the experience from my memory !!!!!

Len E. Huh...you're lucky Jane; I wasn't even the lead tree :)

Terry L. I was Joseph and Karen Miller was Mary! I am now Spartacus.

Brian E. A non-speaking role for me. Wearing a white sheepskin rug pinned across my shoulders, I was a shepherd.

Richie B. I was the woodsman in snow white... Froze as soon as I walked on stage lol...

Pat C. In paper yesterday UK School dropped Nativity Play for a

Cops and Robbers Act! The do-gooders have done it again.

Brian E. The newspapers are very unreliable when it comes to these kinds of stories. Most turn out to be complete fabrications or misrepresentations. Often, a local paper with an axe to grind will report on a local school, and this story is then picked up by a National, such as the Sun.

Pat C. You can blame the Express this time Brian!

Brian E .Well, there you go! Owned by Richard Desmond, who produces almost all of the UK's explicit pornographic magazines and television. He recently lost in the High Court after being sued, but claimed in interviews after he was glad to have won!

Pat C. Yes Brian I saw that he should be a politician.

Penny G. I am attending 2 Christmas concerts next week not sure of the theme not been told as yet should be interesting as last year we had the story of a silly donkey I think

John R. I seem to recall I played the pivotal role of one of the shepherds. While it was a non-speaking part, it was also responsible for bringing the manger onto the stage. For authenticity, we wore an old sheet, with a hole cut in it for our head, and one of my mum's tea towels as head dress. As the Express drama critic commented, "the shepherds delivered a moving performance."

Kim P . I don't remember being in the nativity plays but I was a troll in *The Hobbit* at Bushfield one year. I wanted to be Gandalf but my best mate got the role instead. I think it was a fiendish plot to split us up so we didn't yak in class.

Kim P. Do they still have nativity plays in English schools? Not allowed in USA.

Mark B. I was the donkey at the nursery school nativity in the early seventies, but then I rose up the ranks at infants school to be a Shepherd. My brother was one of the three wise men, with Patrick Atter, can't remember the third wise man though.

Chris G. You'd struggle to find a third one in Wolverton!

I Grew Up in Wolverton Too

Part Three:

Room for the Future

Part Three
Room for the Future

Statues

One of the new statues

June L. Too modern for me.

Faye L. I hate it too x

June L. I didn't think you would want to draw something like that Faye x

Faye L. I'm not June but it does make a good photo lol x

Peter A. Just something else to be left to go rusty like the train wheels outside the old market hall.

Toni B. Whereabouts is this? I like it.... oops !!

Simon C. I like it too!

Peter A. Bottom of the steps leading to Wolverton Park from station hill.

Toni B. Oh thanks Peter. X

Pat G. My grandchildren were asking questions about the wheels outside the Library/Market Hall. They were fascinated by them. Being littleys the wheels seem enormous to them.

Pat G. I like this art piece.

June L. Different Taste to me, I don't think it belongs here in Wolverton like other modern stuff that keeps popping up.

June L. Put it in Central Milton Keynes , not our Old Railway Town.

Pat G. Did you ever see the reclaimed materials art work that was put up at the Radcliffe by the art students there? They were placed all around the old part of the Radcliffe - where the main entrance was. They were quite magnificent - but could be classed as modern too. But if you don't particularly like MK and the modern art around there I can understand that it's intrusion into Wolverton could be a bit much. Last Saturday my husband and I walked along Church Street with 2 of our grandchildren. I was pleased to be able to show my grandson the 'art work' in someone's garden - the green Engine. I was hoping it was still there. My husband said he didn't know about it. Hmm - think his memory is going!

Simon C. But it is next to a modern development! It does also contain Bicycles on the left Arm referencing the parks velodrome!

Pat G. But it is in a 'modern' part of Wolverton ie the houses and apartments built on the old works site. We will have to agree to differ.

Pat G. I didn't like Cofferidge Close in Stony Stratford. Then a friend and her mother came to visit and they pointed out how it did blend in with the old town - they had taken the high entrances of the old coaching inns and incorporated that into the design of Cofferidge Close. Sometimes it takes a different eye to see what has been achieved. As much as we would like things to remain unchanged, unfortunately some things have to change. Saying that - always thought the Agora building was a BIG mistake.

Peter A. I'm sure the cost of this could of been put to better use, to me it's pointless modern or not it stands for nothing other than getting rusty and from the look of it, it's already started to.

June L. I thought it was a skeleton from Faye's cupboard lol

June L. It's escaped Faye as you can see xx

Faye L. I hate that thing its awful. A traditional statue would be better x

Peter A. Could have put a football on the end of his foot might relate a bit more.

Simon C. It was as much a Cycle track as a Football ground back in the 1890's so all good I say! Its great that art is causing debate as it should.

Jackie N. I actually quite like it (and the other similar one down there.....)

Pat G. Do you think people had debate about Rodin's The Walking Man?

Brian E. Yes!

Elaine H. I like it too Jackie. This is a modern area of Wolverton so why not a modern statue?

Chris G. Heres the second...

Faye L. Just when I think they couldn't put up any more

Another metal sculture

eyesores.....

Chris G. I think it's very good very; you have to see it in context and in the 'flesh' rather than a picture taken on a dull day.

Bryan D. Base jumping?

Chris G. Not sure of the significance of this one Bryan, down the arm are bikes over the ages, might be in honour of the velodrome in the old Park but it's only a guess, I'm sure there'll be something in the press this week or next explaining all.

Ian S. It'll probably look a bit better when it rusts away to nothing

Bryan D. When I come up on the 21st, I'll take a look.

Chris G. Stainless steel. When it's still there in a hundred years' time and there is talk of replacing it people on the hologram version of Facebook will meet in virtual reality and demand NOOOOOO! They can't do away with our heritage; they only knocked down our beloved Tesco last week, now this!

Ian S. It's a piece of scrap metal Chris I wouldn't want to wake up to that every day.

Chris G. Your great grandchildren will, living in the olde worlde Park Apartments next door to the monorail stop, London in 10 minutes.

Ian S. Any idea of the cost of this?

Sheila H. Looks Cool.

Chris G. No idea, we're not paying. Its new development. Can't have everything in town looking Victorian.

Ian S. Maybe not directly Chris.

Bryan D. Your prediction yesterday Chris was spot on. I will reserve judgement until I have seen it in its context.

Ian S. I suppose that's why it has a steam train in its hand new and old?

Julia B. I like them, but am a tad worried as metal theft in endemic.

John Rd. It was paid for by PfP and when you look at them from the right angle then it appears they are holding hands...well its meant to anyways...think it was around 25-30k in total...can't remember.

Charlotte L. I live at Wolverton Park and laughed at this when they were putting them up! I don't like them! They should have asked us residents what we thought. I think they are pointless! I know things that get broken e.g. car park shutters seem to take weeks to fix and then they break within the week!!! Also have you seen what someone has done to the door on Hamilton House? Smashed door which was off its hinges and on the floor how someone managed to do that I will never know!! Wonder how long that will take to fix! I hate to say it and I'm not a snob but always seem to happen to the areas where they put the council tenants in.

Ian S. 25 to 30k wasted as far as I am concerned there are still people homeless yet they still are able to find money for these sculptors.

Chris G. But you could say that about beer!

Ian S. Impossible.

John Rd. Well the government for PFP wasting that money as they insist on money for public ;)

Ian S. Regardless of who pays for this I think it's a waste like you say John, the wages were a pittance but there always seems to be a slush fund for this type of project. Personally I think the whole development will be an urban slum in the next 5 to 10 years reading some of these comments on hear it seems its going that way already.

John Rd. And just like any block of flats it will be down to the hundreds of people who live in them, mistreating them. Granted it's not everyone but it is still a majority ruining it for the minority.

Ian S. High density housing does not work people need space to live and breathe.

Bryan D. You're right about that Ian. Don't we ever learn? Many of the high rise blocks that replaced the so-called slums of the 19th century lasted only 30 years before they were bulldozed.

John Rd. The thing is though, coz of the high cost of land, (and in this case the high cost of fixing up the triangle building and lifting shed) developers need to build blocks of flats to make their money back. Wolverton Park cost PFP just over 50 million for 300 residential units and around 30,000 square foot of commercial space. A large number of them residential units are up for rent as well. If not done the exact maths but I do know it will take a very very long time to claw back that investment.

Dave M. Doesn't always work like that though, up here in Leeds and Sheffield many old factories were converted to flats and new blocks seemed to go up every week. Now there are hundreds empty, buyers going bankrupt as they are worth half what they agreed to pay for them. Then there are the management costs which people forget about and if major work is needed it can be in the thousands. Now they are advertised as low rent as they cannot sell them and the poor buggers that did but them end up undesirable's renting them with council benefits which means they are trapped in a hell hole they cannot sell.

John Rd. You get that down here as well. at least this site was built and is being managed by PfP. they also offer 100% mortgage, shared ownership and you can sell back to them within 3yrs at the same price you paid for it. Obviously you lose money on the mortgage interest and in service charges but that's not too bad compared to most places

Dave M. It was the buy to rent speculators that did it up here, paying high prices in the hope of getting high rents. Then when the economy collapsed they tried to back out saying the price is too high but the builders refused to budge and are forcing the buyers to cough up which is sending many to the bankruptcy courts. Greed is a terrible thing.

John Rd. That's what happened up the city centre here as well. And now it's a dive coz they just don't care. the one good thing about Wolverton park is that buy to let is against the lease you sign when you move in. though I do know of one person who was doing it but he was renting to his mates he knew for years and he was still staying there himself a lot so it was allowed in the quiet.

Charlotte L. I'm grateful that Wolverton park did offer 100% mortgages otherwise I'd be saving for the rest of my life and would probably still be living at home! People in the world today have to open their eyes and see the bigger picture sometimes! I think what they have done with Wolverton Park is fantastic turning something run down and horrible and bring it back to life can never be a bad thing! I have lived in Wolverton my whole life and used to play down there as a child. I really can't understand why people hate it so much! There is still so much history about the place and that's wonderful I love walking round and looking at the old and seeing it built within the new! We live in a very modern world now and I think its bloody brilliant! I'm very proud to say I live there! But I do get very angry when people slate it and call it awful etc.

John Rd. I slate Wolverton all the time, I know how bad it is and the surrounding estates but it's still my home town and I love it:

Charlotte L. I would rather live in Wolverton Park then Wolverton itself these days I don't think I feel that safe in Wolverton anymore!

John Rd. No it's safe in Wolverton still.... to be fair. I know some may say there is the odd mugging a burglary but that could happen anywhere. And to be fair most of the people who do the bad things tend to do them to the other bad people ;)

Dale B. I saw this Fine Piece of Craftsmanship Yesterday, as I took a trip from home & decided to go through Wolverton Park, because of all the road works on the Station hill. I understand, it was made from old Railway Tracks & had a little Smile when I saw the Steam train that was clasped in its hand. Great stuff & a big step up from the Concrete cows..!!

John Rd. The posts they stand on have been railways tracks but as for the actual figures are just as likely to be old car panels.

The Royal Train Shed

John Rd. I've got some photos from inside the lifting shed (now called the royal train shed) showing what it looks like now it has been developed into 31 3 story town houses. I will dig them out and put them on here later. Also I heard that the real royal train was never actually kept inside of it and they only called it that in case the IRA decided to sabotage the queen's carriages. Can anyone who perhaps worked the in the 70's & 80's confirm if this is true or not?

Margaret C. My daughter in law Kerry Crew Formerly Wall's Stepdad has driven the Royal train maybe she can find out...

John Rd. When I was working for PFP that train was always being rolled in and out....either the Queen loves her train trips or they are constantly taking it just to stop it going rusty

Margaret C. If I remember right wasn't that long ago that Ron drove it. Mind you he has retired now so won't be doing it again...

Trevor I. On my once a year trip back to Wolverton I always drive by the station/Wolverton park and see all the flats etc. they have built there. Are they nice? Does anyone know anyone who lives in them? Convenient if you commute to London :).

John Rd. I used to work there and to be honest I wouldn't pay the money and you shouldn't either. Even if they do still does the 3 year buy back your losing money in service charge? Buy a 3 bed Terrace in the area for far less money than the cost of a 1 bed flat ;)

Marc H. Where's it kept now I've not seen it going up the line for years as I live 300 yards from the railway

Royal Train Shed

Phillip W. It's still kept in the works it was out just after Xmas
Shell F. Can you go and see it? Or should I say can the public go and see it?
Phillip W. No none can go and see it u can only see it if u catch them taking it in and out of the works
Shell F. Blast as my 9 yr. old son George loves trains and has done since he was 4 it would have made his day to see this xx
Phillip W. You could always see if you and he could visit the works I have been there a few time and is due to go there within the next week to take photos of the site
Shell F. OK I will call them tomorrow and ask thank you
Donna S. Here's a thought.... since the works such a big part of Wolverton's past ... why don't they do guided tours... or do they.... just a thought...
Phillip W. No they don't do that and they won't because Railcare who now use the site is a private company
Shell F. I will suggest it cost the nearest train museum or anything to do with trains that you can go and see is York
Phillip W. It's in Aylesbury
Terry L. Quainton.
Donna S. Well I am of mind that since the works was what it was due to the hard work of the people that worked there.. there would not have been anything viable for this other company to buy and it should be preserved... not to mention they would make money off it... and all businesses love money... I'm just a firm believer in preserving history for after all if not for our pasts we wouldnt be who we are today..

Phillip W. Half the works has gone now anyways and the Railcare rent the buildings and land from another company

Donna S. Well they could still set up some kind of museum surely... have a couple of old railcars.. Something..

Phillip W. No one seem to interested in doing anything like that. I would love to start something up to get the place preserved but no one would be interested and now there is a supermarket on half the works site people would say is there any point.

Maurice H. If you want some ideas of what could be done with it, go see the old GWR works at Swindon.

Wendy C. Any photos of the cinema coach?

Lee P. There's a Wolverton Royal Carriage on display at the Severn Valley Railway Engine Shed, here in Shropshire. It's the one used by George VI and the present Queen. The SVR's well worth a visit, only an hour and a half from Wolverton too.

Why doesn't someone write to the Royal family and tell them the dilemma. Prince Charles has been known to get involved in things in the past, especially if history and community are involved. He may be able to suggest something through the Princes Trust.

Brian E. Is the story we all heard back in the sixties true? Apparently, the Royal Train was taken for a test run down the old Nobby Newport line. A fallen tree branch was sticking out and every single carriage was supposedly scoured the entire length of the train. One story has it that the train was turned around at Newport and the other side similarly scratched, but I suppose that is unlikely as it would not be possible to turn the train around; would it?

Phillip W. Jackie I will try and get a letter put together but I really don't think anything would be done as there is no community spirit in Wolverton left for people to support any plans

Terry L. It was like that when they closed the BCC Fire Station at Wolverton. We thought Royals might intervene when they realised that nearest Fire Station would be Great Holm or Newport Pagnell, and their glorious train might burn down. But nobody cared!!!

Phillip W. Terry do you have any photos of the old fire station

Terry L. Phillip when they closed our Fire Station down, A Whole time crew from Newport Pagnell came whilst we we not at the station and virtually pillaged the station and took all records. So in answer to your question, not many, only the one I posted out the front of the station, and I may have another group photo somewhere but with Eric Mayo on it!

Phillip W. I can't believe they closed the station and then used the building for another car show room

Terry L. Goddard pulled a right flanker by telling us and the council that the building was dangerous and had to be pulled

148

down, all these year later it's still standing and being used as you said as car showroom...

Phillip W. I just can't believe that there was fire station's in Wolverton and now there is none and we really needed to keep it.

Mike W. So where are all the old photos that Wolverton fire station used to have? They must be somewhere? Used to be bigger too including an Ariel ladder truck,

Royal Train Passing Wolverton 1904

Terry L. Photos, probably in Rob Alcocks attic...

I remember when they had a pump escape, the one with a big wheeled ladder on the engine.

Mike W. Now that's a thought, I heard, perhaps wrongly that the dormer window in the back of the appliance bay was to accommodate a turntable ladder, it may have been the pump escape ladder in fairness.

Terry L. Yes it was I can remember Lou Foulkes telling me when I joined up in 1979 Mike Wright.

Mike W. I might have to ask the Newport crews next time I am in.

Terry L. Yes Mike do that for me too please, as that's where they went after leaving Wolverton.

Change at the Station

Chris G. The old Nobby track still there too.

Terry L. Used to spend many hours in that Hut with the station porter Fred..

June E. Its criminal what they've done to that station!

John R. That little hut was also my Grandad's "office" . He was the station porter after he retired as the signalman. The signal box was just the other side of the bridge. If anyone remembers the white haired porter, that was Grandad - some of my best memories are with him and Les (in the ticket office) at the station.

Ian Hs. I remember Bill Westley and a big Mr Wallace. We used to dodge them when train spotting without a platform ticket/ train ticket leg out of the goods yard once the train had gone.

Stairs Leading to the Platform

Constance O. Is that the station in Wolverton?

Terry L. Yep Connie..

Jon H. memories from my childhood it was the portal to far away places, the start of many an adventure

Diane K. Same as Jon, like I said in a previous post I can still hear the sound of me running across those old wooden floorboards in the station couldn't wait to get on the train with dad and off to Lockerbie to see the family, great memories

Mark B. I used to sell newspapers in the morning at Wolverton Staion when I worked for Muscutt and Tompkins just along Stratford Road. The Station always had a distinctive smell, the wooded floorboards, the polished counter at the ticket office, the bike shed off to the right when you walked in. Ah happy days Running up and down those stairs was such fun when we be going or coming back from days out or holidays, Train travel at its best!

Barbara L. Train spotting, collecting details and the Nobby Newport train used to drop coal, local kids suppling their own fire, pleasing mums and dads, nice memories of steam etc.

Jackie N. I can remember it now.........running down the steps when we were off on holiday......and, as Mark mentioned, the smell of the place............

John S. I loved that old Station pity some twit burnt it down.

Kim P. First time I ever went on a train was from here to Bletchley with my mum, I wad probably about 5 or 6. Seemed like such a big adventure at the time.

Kim P. Of course there was no stop at CMK then!

Mark B. Alas John not burnt down but ripped down in an act of vandalism by the Railways own staff, I think your thinking of the Work offices, I sure that was arson (Bloody Tesco's), I was there all night with the fire service as they were worried about the HV cables on the temporary bridge that was there.

Station Entrance with Taxis

Chris G. And taxis too!

Terry L. I remember that mustardy coloured one, think it was a Victor, possibly New City Taxis ?

Chris G. Can remember people running like a bat out of hell off the trains to get one of the handful that were there.

Ron B. Cavalier Terry.

Bryan D. I've just discovered that there may have been a pub on this site prior to 1880. Could've popped in for a pint!

June E. I remember the old station so well, even the smell of the ticket hall, would catch the train regularly to Aspley Guise to see my Nan. Thanks for the memories guys.

June L. I remember as far back as 1950 when I was a child & my mum & dad use to bring me & Bruv Pete for our holidays to stay with my uncle Frank (Chippy) & aunt Hester Watson @ 5 Green Lane Wolverton, lovely memories.

Brian E. Is it true, or merely anecdotal that Wolverton Station interior was once used by a film company as a location in a murder film?

June L. Yes Brian I remember that too.

Brian E. I remember them filming Softly Softly, or whatever Z Cars changed it's name too in Braddel. That was funny - a local woman kept interupting filming.

June L. Wasn't the Film called the Blue Lamp staring Jack Warner, I saw the film, some scenes taken over the Blue Bridge.

Brian E. Was it that one? That's a famous film, it introduced us to Dixon of Dock Green didn't it?

June L. Yes that's right.

Pat B. "The Blue Lamp" 1949 film Starring Jack Warner, Dirk Bogarde (my favourite from the "Doctor" films.) Dora Bryan (Last of the summer wine fame) and many others.

Len E. Slighty off topic, went too see them film a part of the Fourth Protocol, such a time consuming event considering what we saw at the cinema lasted barely a few seconds

Hazel S. In 1949 a film called "The Train of Events" was released and featured a train smashing into a fuel tanker at a level crossing. The location was the western side of the Blue Bridge. Local people were invited to appear as extras on the film set as injured passengers. Jack Warner played a starring role and it was in the following year that "The Blue Lamp" was made.

Pat B. You are right Hazel. "The Blue lamp" was not released until 1950, but according to Halliwells film guide they were both made in 1949. Seems a bit strange for Ealing Studios to have made two similar films so close. They must have had some footage left over.

Ian W. My mum was one of the injured in the train of events but didn't make it to the screen

Chris G. Just looked on Amazon Phil, its available on DVD. Tell the Farm they should have a copy

Lee P. Thanks for confirming what my grandad Jim Knowlson told me. He was an extra in one of the films, I'm assuming Train of Events. Have watched the clips on YouTube but haven't spotted him yet. He'd have been living in Wolverton for less than 2 years when it was filmed, he wasn't demobbed from the RAF (in Jamaica) until late 1947.

Train of Events Film Location 2 March 1949

Brian E. Philip, I think Train of Events was another film parts of which were shot locally. The Green Lamp was not Wolverton, but there is a film from around that time that used the interior of the old station as a setting.

Terry L. Found another "Train of event's" photo today..
Just found this on a website. Somebody may already have put it on but I haven't got time to go through 549 photos tonight!Anne Chapman used to sell the papers there and I would go with her some mornings when I could get up early enough.

Pete B. Ay, this looks nice, better rip it down.

Jackie S. That's how I remember it. All those Saturdays going shopping to Northampton, then later for journeys to London and further.

Brian E. It looks better than I remember it. It was a crime to demolish it as they did!

an Hickson Anybody remember getting platform tickets?

Faye L. It's gorgeous or was rather, I LOVE old buildings like this .

Ian H. ....and lads pushing suitcases down to the station in pushchairs!!

Becca H. I remember the start of many a journey here as a a child. The little ticket office hatch, dad showing the rail passes etc. The

Wolverton Station Entrance

smell of the trains wafting up the stairs - and speaking of the stairs I can almost hear the creak of them They were more worn in the middle from years of use. We wouldn't have known then that we would treasure the memory of just being there. You were just an excited kid, impatiently waiting for the train - with your mum repeatedly telling you to move away from the edge of the platform. It wouldn't matter how long or short your journey was going to be, you just wanted the train to hurry up and come. Walking back up these stairs could be very tiresome to a child with weary legs. Wish I could remember more......

Ian H. I remember looking from the platform towards Castlethorpe where the line bends.............. and waiting for the sound and sight of the steam train, then it came in view,roaring towards us!!

Hazel S. I remember Harry the ticket collector and Sam Hammond also Gordon Parry in the ticket office on one shift and Les on the other.

Donna S. I just remember walking by it everyday to school and home .. bloody hill... ok to go down .. bugger to go up... went to Bletchley a few times and took train for airport to Wolverton the one time we returned as a family for a visit...

Dave P. The annual summer outing was actually the Works shutdown!

Chris G. Top or Bottom Club used to run a big outing via train each year, although it was a family thing I can remember it being

154

a right boozy do with the guards van full of alcohol.

Steve A. Rhyl is one that sticks in my mind.

Chris G. Can remember Portsmouth and Southsea one year too.

Donna S. I can remember going on coach trips, I'm assuming through my dads work at the post office.. lol We'd be 10 mins out of town and I'd be throwing up.. suffered from travel sickness...

Natalie J. omg the memories on here its amazing so sad its changed so much

Jackie S. Why the heck could they not leave the original building and just modernise the carcass to include disabled facilities.

Donna S. because Jackie S. that would require using a braincell.... something these days that seem to be in short supply

Jackie N. That was truly criminal - one day it was there -looked like it was being refurbished -and the next it was gone!

Mike W. You couldn't refurbish it, rose tinted specs off, it was falling down! what would be the point in replacing every bit of timber in the building? would have cost a fortune, more in fact than rebuilding it. without the mass protest, it would have been rebuilt in brick.

Diane R. But the timber might have been OK, it was a lovely building, shame it was pulled down.

Phillip W. The station with all 3 platform buildings.

Chris G. More like a bus shelter type thing on platform one rather than a building as in the model. Must confess don't ever remember it.

A Model of Wolverton's Third Station

John R. Ah, there are the toilets. Do you know when this was taken. I remember the electric wires being put in, but can't remember what year that was.

Julie W. I don't remember it either, but apparently the model was made from an old photo of the station before the 60's xx

Susan H. About 1968 I think - many a holiday started from that station!

Bryan D. I remember them raising the bridge for electrification around 1960, so this photo would be after this.

Hazel S. The first electric trains ran from Euston to the North in test mode on the 12th November 1965 with the full public service being implemented on the 18th April 1966.

Phillip W. There is also a photo from the same book which shows the platform buildings still there in 85

Steve A. All three buildings Phillip ?

Phillip W. Yes, Steve all three unless the date in the book is wrong.

Steve A. It must be Phillip, like Chris I don't remember it at all and as railway lads we were using the train all the time (free travel)

Phillip W. In one of the Bill West books I have the all there after 1970.

Wendy C. Used to love being on this station with my dad when he worked there...

Steve A. Phillip that platform always seemed to be the least used and was usually only pressed into action if there was a problem on one of the other lines. You'd usually only find out at the last minute which then meant a panicked sprint up and over the track.

Chris G. A view down from the old wooden steps down to the Park might explain further if anyone has one or indeed one exists.

Phillip W. True the platform was not that much in it's later years but I know that the building were used. I will try and find out more this week when I am at the museum.

Phillip W. Chris G. one does exist I have seen it on line another photos of that end of wolverton will help too

Chris G. Yep just posted it up Phil and you're spot on, and us local 'experts' will eat humble pie.

Steve A. You live and learn Chris.

Maurice H. Is the old wooden platform No.1 next to the park still there? or did they concrete it?

Phillip W. All the station platforms have now been concreted over

Richard R. This was how I remembered it as a lad!

Julie W. This is a lay out of Wolverton station on display at Milton Keynes model railway exhibition yesterday xx

Richie B. Oh that's amazing

Simon M. Looks good!

Phillip W. Love it that's how the station should look

Colin T. BUT.....That is what it looked like when it was there in the first place, Before the do-gooders pulled the thing down, So now we are turning Street lights off to pay for it to be put back, xx

Steve A. Station hill bend is wrong, it's more off camber than that;) Fantastic bit of model makers though!

Phillip W. A model like this should be placed in the new station

Steve A. I don't recall a waiting room on platform 3, guess there was one when did it disappear?

Steve A. I remember the other two vividly but not on the platform right next to the canal.

Julie W. I don't remember there being a waiting room on the end platform, but this was in the days of steam xx

Phillip W. The platform building were pulled down in the early 1980s

Ron B. That's fantastic

Steve A. I'm talking about the far one Phillip, I have no recollection of there being a building on that platform.

Chris G. Nope there wasn't anything on Platform One, just between 2&3 and then between 4 and 5 where Nobby docked. Great model though.

Phillip W. I have photos of the station were all 3 platforms have waiting rooms on I will try and post them on here later.

Stephen M. Looks how I remember it when I was a lad.

Chris G. The only thing I can remember along that far bank were a building that was something to do the Park, may of course have been something to do with the station years ago.

Wendy C. Should never have been pulled down.

Dorothy S. This map of the old Wolverton rail station is great as we older people remember how it was then.....

Phillip W. Where is incorporated Victorian architecture in this very small looking train station?

Julie W. It looks bloody awful xx

Phillip W. I know but this is what people want now days

Chris G. But it imitates an old railway workshop in style?

Pete B. Oh yes they both have roofs on ...

Phillip W. It kind of does yeah but it's in the wrong place and too small but I suppose we r lucky to finally have in

Chris G. Given how the station has survived with just a tin hut and a lean too roof for years not sure its too small for the amount of custom that goes through there each day. Lets wait and see what the finished article is like, it is after all still a building site.

Phillip W. True I hope the finish station will look good

Jackie S. I know I don't live there anymore, but I am a great believer in progress and modernisation. I hate it. Yes, it is a modern building and it has modern facilities, I assume, but who the hell is employing these architects who are totally unsympathetic to the history and character of a place.

Chris G. But it is, it mirrors the old railway workshops.

Phillip W. the station was supposed to be made to look like old one and put in it's place at the top of the hill

The New Station at Wolverton

Wolverton Station in the days of Steam

Chris G. Not sure that ever in the plan Phil nor financially would it be feasible.

Phillip W. it was in a plan a few years ok but it got changed some where along the line

Chris G. Probably due to cost if it was.
Phillip W. yep that sounds right.

Rubbish Collection Day

Clean Up Wolverton

Phillip W. Here's a question how many people on here would like to have Wolverton the railway town back all cleaned up all local shops reopened and the town history celebrated not forgot about.
John C. Sounds good to me.
Phillip W. Railcare and Wolverton groups should get together and try and bring the town communities together for another big celebration like the Wolverton 150.
Karen W. Would love to see it!!!!
Jane B. I'd love to see it - but I think we all know it isn't going to happen !!!!
Helen P. How could that happen???
Jackie S. Community involvement?
Chris G. Not me, I think there's an awful lot of rose tinted views on what a lovely place Wolverton was, times change.
Ian H. Chris, of course Wolverton can never be the same again, however I suggest that everyone on here would wish it could be. Nostalgic maybe, factual sure but rose-tinted hardly, in my view

of the comments posted.

Chris G. I'm talking about the fabric of the town Ian not the sense of community or our memories of growing up or indeed the people. Wolverton was a small industrial town, some aspects do need preserving but nowhere near all of it. There has to be progress and new life or the town will die through lack of it. Purely my opinion of course but I think sometimes we think preservation is about bringing back the good old days nut its not its about living in a museum. The good old days were the people, the characters and yes who did what to whom, sadly something we cannot preserve.

Ian H. Well put Chris I obviously misconstrued your post. Entirely agree.

Andrew L. I'd like to see it thrive, with shops and jobs and for the schools to be as good as they were.

Ian W. Could we live without Tesco's or would we all desert Wolverton for Bletchley supermarkets?

Pete B. It could be as it was pre 1970 but I can not get my time machine to work!!!

Wendy Ch. Think we need a Tardis

Chris G. I'm sure we would Ian or shop online. With so much more going on in modern life the majority of folks just don't have the time or indeed the inclination to traipse round half a dozen shops when it can all be found in one store.

Phillip W. We do then I could go back in time and take loads of photo's and see my grandpa.

Maurice H. Not just Wolverton, but all the little villages that have been wiped out by the leviathan called Milton Keynes. How much other history have we lost thanks to so called Progress?

Phillip W. So would I but I am more into the history of Wolverton and the works and seeing what it all looked like.

Sylvia A. Although I agree it is essential that we progress and move forwards I think its great to remember the history of our home towns. That's why this FB page is such an incredible and amazing idea. Nostalgia does tend to leave out any bad times and bad memories, but a reunion of Wolverton town folk maybe in the summer at one of the recs or clubs would be an excellent idea. people could bring photos and share meories and maybe bump into someone they haven't seen for years. Wolverton can never be the same as it was in the past....even if we reopened all the same old shops etc ...its the people that create the lovely memories and so many of them have moved on, and the fond memories we have now are based on our perspective at the time. Such a shame however that Wolverton has not just progressed but has lots its wonderful sense of inclusive community that it once had.

Donna S. I agree with what Sylvia said. ... while would be a fantastic idea it was a moment in time for all of us from our generation and older. you cant get that back... as I was raised to believe a house is just a house, its the people inside it that make it a home , same is true of a community. and the people that made Wolverton the way we fondly remember are gone . and I'm sorry but todays generation(not all, but quite a few) really don't know what a sense of community is ... all they worry about is ... i want something and i want it now . thats why i like where i live .... small community, small businesses and everyone says good morning... for so many years didn't have that .. but it would be so cool to get all the small shops open again... get the square back to what it used to be ...

Phillip W. But it would be nice for Wolverton to be made nice and have more about it's history on display for our children's children.

Deborah B. A great thought but isn't going to happen.

Phillip W. The footprints of the building that where pulled down for Tesco should at least be marked out seems they going to waste money by pulling down the store they have even though the toilets have not long been done up what a waste of money.

Transformation in our Times

Forty years ago the rhythms of the day were punctuated by the sight of thousands of workers filling the Stratford Road. The main gate symbolised the dominance of the Railway Works. Some workshops remain, employing about 100 people. Tesco now occupies the site of the original workshops and a good part of the main office buildings. Would people rather keep this or settle for Tesco?

Ruth E. Well I loved, and still do, shopping in a variety of shops. That way the community stays in touch,but I do shop in Supermarkets and have no real objections to them. Shall stand back at a safe distance now Bryan! xxx

Philip E. Should never been pulled down.

Gloria S. Love this picture, it pulls at the heart strings. But time moves on. Wolverton must update or it will die.

Soraya T. I'd rather have this if it was used and viable but we don't live in a world where we can have everything.

Mark Simm Should've used it as Tesco.

Sue R. Should have been kept as it was!

Rachel J. I agree with Mark and Gloria. Wolverton needs a good rejuvenation project to take Wolverton forward. Bletchley is an example of this, (MK1, Dons etc, and now a new cinema being built!) Come on Wolverton don't die.

Chris G. Hmmmm Tesco thanks, its of use to the people of the

BR Main Gate

town in the present, rather than living in a museum of an idealised past. Perhaps if Facebook existed 175 years ago someone might have posted a pic of a field of sheep with rolling views down the Ouse Valley and asked, what do you prefer, this or a railway works?

Steve H. Call me sentimental but I'd rather have the Wolverton of old.

Terry Lt. Me too Steve.

Adrian C. I love the old pics of Wolverton , but we have to look to the future wherever we live. Problem is do these huge supermarket chains put the smaller supermarkets out of business ie Budgens, Dudney and Johnsons etc? Here in Aus. The 2 big supermarket chains, Coles and Wolworths, have put out of business many local shops and control the costs of such things as bread and milk. Bugger, I think I've digressed and got on my high horse. Apologies

Peter A. No reason to demolish history to move forward. Rejuvenate more like re-populate. Much prefer the old.

Chris G. I'd agree with that Pete re the use of old buildings but sometimes its just not practical or cost effective.

Adrian C. At least keep the fascia of the old buildings

Chris G. Titch, and you don't think the shopkeepers of old didn't control prices over their captive audience in small towns such as Wolverton?

Adrian C. Of course they did. They have to make a profit (capitalism). Our supermarkets are selling milk at $2 a litre forcing the local corner shops out of business, do want your retail market

162

controlled by these huge chains? Next the local Co-ops will be squeezed out.

David M. I'm all for saving old buildings of historic interest or architectural merit, but in my opinion those had neither, they were just plain ugly. Having said that I can understand a nostalgia for Wolverton as we remember it in the long gone days of our youth, but those days are sadly gone and retaining any old buildings for the sake of it will not change that. I have recently suggested to my GP that I would like to cancel old age and return my bus pass, unfortunately it seems that this is not allowed. As to Tesco being a suitable replacement, that is a separate question. Certainly Wolverton needs to move with the times to survive and that certainly means shopping facilities of that sort... and yes, I know that we we would all like to see the return of the old shops like King's bakery, but then how many of us continued to shop there when Tesco opened.

Adrian C. Very valid point David. I was back recently and did the bulk of my shopping at Tescos.

Peter A. I shopped at Cole's in salamander bay regular not alot of difference between that and Tesco but liked the idea of segregating the alcohol giving it it's own little outlet in the corner and the way it was stored. As you say Adrian they put the squeeze on the smaller shops eventually killing them off.

David M. Same applies to the DIY shops. Homebase and B&Q etc. have killed off most of the small ironmongers and tool suppliers so that many specialised items which don't sell in sufficient volume are removed from the shelves, it then follows that it ceases to be worthwhile for the manufacturers to produce them and they disappear altogether

Chris G. But like it or not its the consumer that drives change, if people didn't shop at supermarkets they wouldn't build them, times change. I think a generation on and the kids of today may look back on the quaint old supermarkets that disappeared when everyone hit the buy button on the internet and everything was delivered to your doorstep. No so different from Terry Levitt on Sam Tuckeys butcher bike.

David M. That's right Chris, we get what we ask for!

Mike W. They were industrial buildings, old and unsuitable for modern industrial use. Imagine if the works had stayed open? All the old buildings would be gone, replaced by modern, efficient ones. Some of the site would still have been sold and commercially developed. Sadly, this is progress. Wolverton of today looks good. its the loss of community not the buildings'

Rachel J. Mike you hit the nail on the head,

Stephen Ce. Should have tried to adapt older buildings and kept some history.

Bryan D. I put this up this morning in the hope of a variety of responses - and thank you. The fact remains that Wolverton has always been subject to change. Even if you put aside the loss of the castle, all medieval buildings, the great Elizabethan house that was 140 feet long, the disappearance of most 17th to 19th century farmhouses you will find that the Wolverton that came into being 175 years ago has almost vanished. The process started early. Three streets were eliminated in the 1850s. All of the streets north of the Stratford Road had gone by 1900. Two gas works in different locations preceded the third on the Old Wolverton Road. Similarly, two early station buildings had gone by 1881. There was a 3 storey losing house on the site now occupied by Madcap in the 1850s. That lasted about 10 years. The Little Streets and the Gables were flattened in the 1960s and I have to tell you that no tears were shed at the time. In fact when a group of metropolitan newcomers campaigned to save a block on Spencer Street, most locals thought they were crazy. We have a tendency to put on our rose-tired glass as we look back on the past. A harmless enough indulgence but would we really want to go back to living in uninsulated houses heated by dirty and inefficient coal fires, gas lamps, daily shopping for small amounts of food, reduced life expectancy?

Chris G. One thing, I bet those living above the shops etc on the south side of Stratford Rd have a much clearer and brighter outlook now

John R. We all tend to look at the past through rose tinted glasses, but in retrospect, we live in a much better environment now than we grew up with in Wolverton as kids. While Tesco's and the like prosper, they do so because they fill a need that wasn't met by the small business - as Chris said, if people didn't shop there, they wouldn't be in business. Will our kids and grandkids be looking back lamenting the passing of these types of businesses that have now been replaced by a futuristic online personalized shopping service - sure they will, that's progress.

Susan B. When we were little there was no Sunday trading either, when it first came in, I wonder how many of us said no we wouldn't go shopping as its a rest day, I enjoyed living in Wolverton when I was younger with the small corner shops and butchers and the Friday market in Creed St. I took my dad shopping the last time I stayed in Wolverton, I was remembering what shops was along Church Street and Stratford Rd. I know time has gone by and we have to live in the future, but it is a shame that some of the bigger stores took over the smaller shops and made them closed

Tasha B. I think its sad how Wolverton has had to change so much thry could have keep more buildings.

Terence S. The problem is that times have changed and people no longer work 9-5. I find myself doing a main shop when I have just finished nights. However Tesco quality isn't as good as it used to be. Wish we had an Aldi/Lidl in Wolverton. Quality is good and price is cheaper than Tesco.Wolverton Bucks I'll take a HS2 supporting business occupying some of the site north of the wall, and investment to bring it up to state of the art.

Michael M. Interesting thought Terence, the quality of products comes at a price (but who's ?) I had opportunity to compare Animal welfare standards in the cooked meat industry. Believe it or not the big 4 supermarkets find it hard to challenge the costs of the supply chain in Europe such as a German supplier as on the whole these companys purchase from supply lines that have lower welfare standards, being British stiff upper lip and all that we stuff our farmers with the highest standards and costs around then as consumers we expect to pay peanuts. Lidl have in my opinion the cheapest and the best 400g dry cured waferthin ham in the UK real cost Animal welfare. Use a British supplier and to match costs the quality in production and added water becomes the norm.

Adrian C. Wow, what a can of worms we've opened, but the underlying fact is that we all pretty much agree on the same thing, where-ever we are in the world. All started by an old picture of Wolverton .

Michael M. I love this site! great topic's who know where they lead. Reconnected with some old school mates as well. Get stuck in Adrian! pic are good too

Jennifer T. Brill pic, just l remember it a a teenager in the 60s.

Hilary S. Wolverton as it was happy memories.

Wolverton's Progress

Phillip W. Years ago Wolverton was a nice little railway town with green fields. now look at it houses being put on any free green field empty shops the town is looking in need of help. who is going to be living in all these new houses....

Jackie S. Whoever they are, they probably won't care about the past.

Phillip W. You're right there. As I have found out over the last few days there is not a lot of people who are interested in the history of the town

Vicki L. It's very sad, I drive by thinking how Wolverton was!! Same here in Stony, any empty land is snapped up & built on!! They won't stop until there is no green land left!!

Phillip W. That's just what I was thinking it's like with the little bit of land behind mine next to Electrolux they want to put house for 11 households on it but the land is not big enough but I bet that

wont stop them

Chris G. You're too young to remember Philip but bar the two Recs you weren't legally allowed on any of the other land by and large. For all the slagging off of MK here we have far more recreational land and parks in the area than we ever had in the 'good old days' As for the town being nice well that's a matter of perspective, in my mind in what a grubby little industrial south midlands town, the people and sense of community may have made it but preserving buildings for the sake of it will never ever bring that back. As for new houses well they are not built for the fun of it and builders and developers are not stupid, there clearly is a demand for them. And people are interested in the history of the town by and large its just that not many of us want to live in it.

Phillip W. But there are still empty places in Wolverton park and in the new houses in church street I think they to build place of employment first.

Wolverton Park Development

Chris G. I should point out I meant living in the past (history) not living in the town.

Phillip W. I don't mean living in the past but to much of building from the past are being pulled down and replaced by crap looking things why not build within the old but again why housing when is loads of empty house and no one can afford to buy them.

Ian S. Oh! come on Chris speak your mind

Andrew L. Wolverton terraces made of brick and slate are over 100 years old now may be tatty, but I would be happy to bet (if I could live long enough to win the bet) that the terraces will still be there when the new-builds on the Print site are demolished.

There is no chance of me ever being happy to buy a shell with egg-box material stud walls and cheap as possible fittings. There's a difference between real progress and money-grabbing developments.

Chris G. But bar the little streets no terrace housing has gone. Economics dictates building materials and the time taken to build nowadays and coastwise building a three bed semi against a Victorian fully brick three bed terrace would be a fair difference in sale price. Which would sell quicker, well as with everything the cheaper one.

Brian E. Back in the early seventies, when MKDC was still in the early stages of creating the new city, houses in Wolverton were very desirable & were being snapped up by first time buyers, many of them in the building trade. Then, people were gutting the interiors, throwing out original fire places and panel doors, and creating open plan by demolishing interior walls. Just look at Stacey Bushes as an example of how tacky modern houses are by comparison. I can remember all those early estates around Wolverton & Stratford going up, and most were housing problems and problem estates just waiting to happen.

Bryan D. Good point Brian. My brother bought the house we grew up in and energetically set about "modernising" it. The thing he most regretted was taking out the heavy wooden doors and replacing them with the then trendy panel doors. So he transformed a house that had fairly good sound insulation to one where you could hear every squeak from anywhere in the house.

Bryan D. I'm broadly with you on this one Chris. Progress is generally beneficial and represents what most people want. The houses on Cambridge St and Windsor St, for example, represented a progressive development in housing from, say, Buckingham St. And if you asked those who formerly lived in Ledsam Street if the were better off being moved to Woodland View, I bet you would have got a positive response. Would I like to continue shopping for my groceries at corner shops and spend one third of my income on food or would I rather go to Tesco and spend only 18 per cent? I'm interested in the history of Wolverton and I have sentimental feelings towards it but I would have to note (along with many others on this group) that I no longer live there. There have been a lot of mistakes in Wolverton's development and some of them started very early. Three new streets, for example, were bulldozed only 15 years after they were built. The Royal Engineer (the oldest pub 1841) was only built because they made a mistake in the location of the first one. There was a large lodging house on Creed St where Madcap now is. Built in the 1850s; torn down by 1870. I could go on, but enough.

Brian E. I had friends in Victoria Street at the time, who inherited a house. I helped him remove the Victorian fireplace, re-set the hearth, and re-install the whole thing as it was. The previous occupants has 'open-planned' the house, but up & down the street people were chucking original doors and fittings into skips! So, we were able to reclaim what we needed from the trendy new buyers up the road and restore the house to it's original condition

Mike L. Totally agree Bryan, but when there isn't a butcher in the town that isn't Halal and all of the women's clothes shops are only selling Saris there is surely something wrong!

Jane B. Couldn't agree more.

Mike L. - the whole fabric of what Wolverton once was has gone - and we'll never get it back - so whilst I hanker after the town that I grew up in I realise that it has gone forever - so suppose we need to adapt to what we have now - even thought most of us "oldies" hate it - think it's called "Progress" !!!!

Chris G. Why is that wrong if that reflects the populace of the town now? Perhaps when some of look at that perceived great community we all grew up they might want to look at those that sold up and moved away for their displeasure rather than those that moved into the area to fill the void created by those that left town. As far as I know nobody left screaming and kicking.

Jane B. What you say makes a lot of sense Chris (okay, I'm grovelling here) - but seriously, you and I are still in the town and have seen the gradual downturn of the community - whilst I don't like it at all I realise that if I want to stay in the

town I've grown up in then I need to change with it !!! Saying that, I moan about it like everyone else - but hey, I'm still here, so that must say something !!! Jeez, I've just turned into my Mother !!!!

Maryanne L. Yes, but how far do you have to go to get meat from an English butcher (excluding Tesco). Who's catering for the original community?

Chris G. That's economics though Mike, if there was money to be made by an 'English' butcher as with any other commercial outlet one would surely exist. But then that's nothing to do with an influx of people, that's down to that 'original' community

shopping elsewhere, mostly for convenience at places like Tesco. And maybe just maybe is a large chunk of that original community had stayed in the town then a butcher might still be in trade, though somehow I doubt it. The new butchers in the town are not the problem, the problem is the people who left.

Becca H. How far did you have to go to find a major chain supermarket before there was a Tesco with all its convenience that I presume no-one currently living in Wolverton takes advantage of. Did we all go into the details of how the meat and poultry we bought was killed and prepared when there was a so called

English Butcher? Why and when did the former 'butcher shut and cease trading. etc etc.

Mike L. - its not just a simple question of being passive and wondering why things isn't what they used to be and - who exactly are the "original community" that have these specific needs that have been denied of late?

Deborah C. Well I certainly didn't leave Wolverton kicking and screaming - however I love its diversity now compared to the small Scottish town where I now live that has none - I'd definitely come back if I could!

Mike L. Chris G., the people that left would include me, but some of my family still live there. If I go to a butcher here and ask for pig's liver or lamb's heart I've had the reply 'there's no call for it' - but I've just asked for it, so there must be a call for it. There are still people in Wolverton that have a call for an English butcher.

Becca H. Well maybe if it is such a strong and popular call we could go almost right back to the beginning and get these people together to form a co-operative - and open an English Butchers! It could be called the CO-OP - but I think that name has

already been snapped up by another trader! Can you get these items in Tesco? and if so is there nothing wrong with them - just because they come out of a big shop that also happens to sell other stuff?

Chris G. There may be a call but not enough of a call to make one economically viable. If there was someone would tap into that market. Why doesn't one exist, there are empty shops in Wolverton to service one if there was a demand. Just because halal butchers exist doesn't mean any other type cannot in Wolverton. No one is going to run one at a loss though surely? Like I said before its all about economics, supply and demand. Clearly there is just not that level of demand anymore to make one viable. On the other hand for halal meat there clearly is and butchers exist to service that market, but you do have to ask yourself if Tesco sold it, would there be?

Dave M. Hate to disappoint but apart from Morrison's all other supermarkets meat is halal.

Andrew L. I'm all for progress myself, but having grown up in a Wolverton terrace, and then bought my first house - an MK new build, I don't actually see any progress in housing. I couldn't wait to get away from the cheap and as flimsy as the builders could get away with construction and fittings that just fell apart.

Bryan D. ...The supermarket hadn't been invented when I was growing up in Wolverton, nor had packaging, which makes self service shopping possible. Nor did many people have cars or fridges so shopping had to be local and frequent. Gradually our society changed and the supermarket is probably a good measure of how it did change. Chain grocery shops like Dudeney and Johnston started to spread in the region. The Co-op introduced self service shopping. Smaller groceries tried to fight the tide with affiliation to Spar and Wavy Line, but the trend was inevitable. Budgens (which now appears quite small) introduced one-stop shopping and inevitably the supermarket giants swallowed up everything. The choice I make, and it's an inevitable one, is to take the convenience, range of products, and lower price of Tesco rather than the cheery smile, limited product range and higher price of a local shop. Sorry, but there it is. Wolverton has always been subject to change. The Wolverton that I grew up in looked timeless and stable, but in reality that was the Wolverton I encountered at that point in time. From 1838 new people came in, some with strange accents and some even with religious affiliation that had been unknown in Wolverton for 150 years. I mean Roman Catholics. In time they got their own church and settled into the community. Throughout its history Wolverton has always been a magnet. There was work and it was fairly well paid. In the last decade there has been a new and visible influx which has created a demand for shops selling saris and kaftans and halal meat. So be it. They are still Wolverton people. In 2052 you might hear this remark: "Wolverton's not the same any more Abdul. They closed the old mosque and now the town is full of Jedi Knights."

Dave M. We are lucky in that our village has several small stores, two selling food, a bakery, fruit & Veg and a hardware store. So I do most of the shopping locally when walking the dog. However would be too limited and expensive to do all of it that way so still do the 'Big Shop' at a supermarket (not Tesco though - hate their stuff).

Phillip W. The thing that gets me about Tesco is the fact that they spent lots of money doing up their toilet only to flatten the shop in a year what's the point

Dave M. Oh and Bryan near by here in Sheffield there are several areas that used to be very select 20 odd years ago, but the large Victorian houses were snapped up by large Asian families and eventually became exclusive to them. They are now run down uncared for, non-white and undesirable to any other race. Integration is one thing and would be well and good but that is not what happens.

Bryan D. I guess most people's observations on this thread are right, Dave. There is a lost past to be mourned and sometimes we have to wonder what we gained from "progress".My general point was that change does happen and we might as well acknowledge get it and get on with life. A lot of change in my lifetime has been driven by technology and n the domestic front this has had a huge impact. I'll leave people to judge whether or not it's good or bad.

The other type of change you alluded to is political, where our masters decided for ideological reasons to encourage immigrants to transplant their culture here without any recognition of the indigenous culture, mainly, I understand, because we were beastly to them in our imperial past.

Chris G. Or on the other hand at successive periods we've needed an influx of cheap labour to do jobs the indigenous (and that can only be a very loose term) didn't or wouldn't do.

Bryan D. Yes I used to think that sleepers were ties that held down the railway track until I saw all the photos on the Wolverton Works Group. :-)

Dave M. I think they were quite capable on their own Bryan, we are slagged off because of imperialism, however Kenya used to be safe and Zimbabwe used to be the garden of Africa. Whilst crime was always there we didn't have armed Somalia and west Indian drug gangs, Romanian pickpockets etc. I suspect this is what people really miss a place where crime was low and your neighbour was a friend. Of course like myself, Terry and others you can move out to the countryside and for the most part separate yourself from the sad reality of the world today.

Bryan D. To the Country! 50 years ago I wouldn't have considered it, but now . . . Well, it's still a bit of England. Oddly enough, in the light of my earlier comments, our present house used to be the village grocery, which did a reasonable business until Tesco built its Supermarket two miles away in about 1985. The lady who used to own it told me that once Tesco opened they used to send someone down every day to check on her prices. Before too long she was out of business.

Dave M. Luckily for the villages round here all the supermarkets are in Sheffield itself and trying to negotiate the traffic means not planning much else for the day, so they are well used. People mock the roundabouts in MK but they want to try traffic lights every 50 yards that are only on green for 20 seconds.

not to forget bus gates, one way systems trams that have centre road blocks at every stop so you can't get past etc etc - better stop now feel road rage coming on !!

Bryan D. Careful Dave! Sounds like you need a relaxing pint at your local.

The Old and the New

Pete B. The old and the new. Wolverton needs change , but will the new last as long as the old did?

Ant K. I fear not !

171

Darren S. Def not

Jackie N. It certainly won't last as long !

Chris G. But if the people who built the bit on the left hadn't also rejuvenated the bit on the right it wouldn't have lasted much longer either, payoff I guess.

Canal Development

June L. No way. I had a Guest House in Wolverton for 17years & accommodated Shelf fitters,builders,Tree planters Prison Officers all sorts because they were coming in from everywhere to work in MK but there wasn't enough B&B to accommodate them all.

Pat G. I have a sense that my new house (about 7 years old) will not last as long as the house I lived in in Gloucester Road. I don't know why really - perhaps just the different building methods. However, I do know that the insulation etc is much better than the older houses. And the house I lived in in Stony Stratford was not built very well at all. The term 'Jerry-built' springs to mind. It is still standing but probably because it is held up by the houses on either side of it!

Wolverton Park Today

Remembrance Day

As we go to press with this volume it is worth noting that one thing that hasn't changed over the last 95 years is our respect for the fallen in the wars of the 20th century, and of course those of present conflicts.

Chris G. It's Remembrance weekend, we all mark it in our own way, for me though I'll always think of these words by Hawtin Munday. He's not some well heeled writer or war poet, just a local lad called up to fight, spent his life in Bradwell and like most of us locals worked in Wolverton Works. These are his thoughts after getting caught in no mans land and tending for a dying comrade before being captured as a prisoner of war.

"So I kept lighting fags for him, and later in the afternoon he called again. I went to him and he got his old fag tin out, put a fag in his mouth, and then he said, ''Ere you are', with his fag tin. He says, ''Ere kid, you have these fags,' he said, 'I shan't want 'em. He said, 'If you ever get out of this, he said, 'tell me mum won't you?' I says, 'Yes I'll tell her, I'll tell her'. Well I couldn't, I didn't know who he was. I couldn't tell. I says, 'Yes I'll tell her'. Well within a minute or so of that, I lit his fag, it dropped out of his mouth and he said, 'Oh God, help me'. And that was the end of that."

"Well, then I turned round and looked across No-Man's-land.

Well all along No-Man's-land , there wasn't a shot being fired, but it was lit up like daylight because all the time, you see, from their trenches and our trenches they kept firing Star shells and that lights up like electric lights in the sky. Well, when we looked across there you could see all our blokes laying dead, all over the place, it was lit up as clear as that. If only a artist, a well known

The Old Cenotaph in the Square

artist, could have only have stood there with us and painted that scene as it was there and they'd took it back and hung it in the rooms or cabinet headquarters of other countries, they never dared declared another war, if they sat and looked at that, and I know, I'm certain - if they could have put all the colouring in you know, the blokes,Germans, in between the first and second line of theirs, and ours laying about, they daren't have declared a war, not if they'd got any sense and see that hanging up."

"Years later, when we got old, my old darling, she always used to read the Good Book before we went to sleep, you know. What I can recall mainly was the little bit she used to read; 'As I pass through the valley of the shadow of death I will fear no evil'. Now then, I always remembered that, you see and the old dear used to read it and I used to say then, ' I did pass through the valley of the shadow of death, and I felt no evil'."

Linda R. This is lovely Chris. I remember Hawt Munday and took my mum and dad to see Days Of Pride. He was a special old man with a fantastic memory and a brilliant way with words xx
Ian H. Thanks for this Chris.
Jane B. Good post Chris - let's remember those who gave their lives for us xxxx
Anna O. So many stories/accounts of experience have been lost.... I heard many as I was growing up but sadly did not pay so much attention then - we need to record them and pass them on now to our young people. My mums generation have nearly all passed on now but they were all such strong people... principally made so from their wartime experiences.
Jacqui R. My granddaughter is being taught all about the last wars at junior school at the moment , have been sending photos and information to her recently x it's not before time either all schools should be bringing it into the curriculum, after all it is history!! x
Jackie N. I remember Mum and Dad going to "Days Of Pride -at the end of the show it was announced that Hawtin was in the audience!-not a dry eye in the house....
Steph M. That brought tears to my eyes - why oh why the terrible loss of life? We will remember them.
Vicki M. I used to go to Mr and Mrs Munday's with mum when she cut Mrs Munday's hair. They were devoted to each other and the loveliest people. My dad always said Hawtin Munday was "a good old boy": the highest of praise coming from him.
Pat G. The wars have been on the history curriculum for some years now. This is a great post Chris.
Jackie N. Lots of visits by secondary schools planned to the first world war sites in Belgium etc:next year, as part of the remembrance of 100 years . We need to make sure the next generation never forget too........
Rod H. My Granddad was a Friend of Hawtin, & I used to go with gramp regular to visit him, very interesting to listen to them talking.

Postscript

This busy car park was originally occupied by residential housing and workshops. By the end of the 19th century the space and the area continuing half a mile westward was taken up by railway workshops and offices. This was still recognisably the Wolverton of the mid 20t century. But nothing ever stands still and that Wolverton had largely gone by the beginning of the 21st century.

This transformation has occurred in the lifetime of all of the contributors to this volume and it is our intention to record not merely the change itself but the effect that it has had on Wolverton the community.

In these pages there has been some grumbling, a good deal of realism, and some celebration of the change. As a collection of conversations the book is inevitably uneven, but we believe, an authentic portrayal of that change from the people who have lived through it and with it.

175 years ago the photographer would have been standing in the middle of a great construction site that became the first engine shed, surrounded by terraced streets. The only remnants of those early years are part of the school building on the right (1840) and the church spire (1844). Wolverton has moved on.

Index to Contibutors

Valerie Davies	Valerie D.	Mark Hampson	Mark H.
Sarah Day	Sarah D.	Gaynor Hancock	Gaynor H.
Jane Deeks	Jane D.	Jacqui Hartley	Jacqui H.
Jenny Denton	Jenny D.	Susan Hay	Susan H.
Andrew Dix	Andrew D.	Eddie Hayes	Eddie H.
Tricia Downes	Tricia D.	Colin Hayle	Colin H.
Hazel Drinkwater	Hazel D.	Becca Hemmerman	
			Becca H.
Brian Eakins	Brian E.	Steve Hepworth	Steve H.
Philip Edwards	Philip E.	Ian Hickson	Ian H.
Len Eccles	Len E.	Sheila Higginbotham	
David Emery	David E.		Sheila H.
June Emery	June E.	Jenifer Hobbs	Jennifer H.
		Ian Hockings	Ian Hs.
Pam Farmer	Pam F.	Debbie Hodder	Debbie H.
Helen Fisher	Helen F.	Lisa Holman	Lisa H.
Lee Foote	Lee F.	Edith Holyhead	Edith H.
Shell French	Shell F.	Elaine Hudson	Elaine H.
Pat Fryatt	Pat F.	Maurice Hunt	Maurice H.
Phillip Gammage	Phillip G.	Trevor Iles	Trevor I.
Jill Garrett	Jill G.		
Penny Glasgow	Penny G.	Natalie James	Natalie J.
Chris Gleadell	Chris G.	Rachel Jennings	Rachel J.
Stephen Godfrey	Stephen G.	David Jolley	David J.
Katie Goodridge	Katie G.	Brian Jones	Brian J.
Lin Goodwin	Lin G.		
Martin Grant	Marin G.	Nahida Kassam	Nahida K.
Roy Green	Roy G.	Bob Kelly	Bob K.
John Grey	John G.	Danny Kelly	Danny K.
Jacqueline Grey	Jacqueline G.	Gary Kelly	Gary K.
Patsy Griffin	Patsy G.	Julie Kely	Julie K.
Colin Griffiths	Colin G.	Sarah Kelly	Sarah K.
Gareth Griffiths	Gareth G.	Diane Kent	Diane K.
Jean Grogan	Jean G.	Linda Kincaid	Linda K.
		Ant King	Ant K.
Molly Hagan	Molly H.	Susan King	Susan Kg.
Tim Hague	Tim H.	Susan Kirton	Susan K.
Sarah Hampshire	Sarah H.	Andrew Labrum	Andrew Lm.

Geoff Labrum   Geoff L.
Andrew Lambert Andrew L.
Ian Lawson   Ian L.
Sue Leacock   Sue L.
Charlotte Legg Charlotte L.
Barbara Levitt Barbara L.
June Levitt   June L.
Pete Levitt   Pete L.
Terry Levitt   Terry L.
Brian Lewis   Brian L.
Billy Lisle   Billy L.
Faye Lloyd   Faye L.
Mike Lloyd   Mike L.
Graham Lloyd   Graham L.
Julie Locke   Julie L.
Pamela Lockett Pamela L.

Sheila Mabey   Sheila M.
Lynette Mallows Lynette M.
David Marks   David M.
Doug Marshall   Doug M.
Elaine Martin   Elaine Mn.
Stephen Martin Stephen M.
Steph Mather   Steph M.
Jane Maxey   Jane M.
Julie Maxey   Julie M.
Ian McKenzie   Ian M.
Elizabeth McMillan
                Elizabeth M.
John McSherry   John Mc.
Maria Miceli   Maria M.
Dave Millard   Dave M.
Clare Moody   Clare M.
Mason Moore   Mason M.
Simon Moore   Simon M.
Pauline Morgan Pauline M.
Elaine Morley   Elaine M.
Aimée Morris   Aimée M.

Andy Morris   Andy M.
Rosa Mule Buscalgia
                Rosa B.
Janice Myers   Janice M.
John Myers   John M.
Susan Nicholson Susan N.

Jane Neal   Jane N.
Andrew Norton   Andrew N.
Jackie Nott   Jackie N.

Donnah Oakey   Donna O.
David Old   David O.
Sylv Olver   Sylv O.
Chris Owens   Chris O.
Constance Owens
                Constance O.

Kathy Paice   Kathy P.
Julie Palmer   Julie P.
Steve Palmer   Steve P.
John Parker   John P.
Helen P. Helen P.
Kim Pavey   Kim P.
Dave Pjillips   Dave P.
Elaine Pilcher Elaine P.
Bev Pinkerman   Bev P.
Carol pointer   Carol P.
Gary Pooley   Gary P.
Jon Pooley   John P.
Cate Prescott   Cate P.
Craig Preston   Craig P.
Lee Proudfoot   Lee P.
Emma Pullen   Emma P.

Edward Quinn   Edward Q.

Lynsey Rainbow Lynsey R.
Del Ratcliffe   Del R.

John Reed	John Rd.	Sheila Stone	Sheila S.
Lynn Reeves	Lynn R.	Lee Ann Styles	Lee Ann S.
Diane Richards	Diane R.	Elaine Sullivan	Elaine S.
Pina Ricioppo	**Pina R.**	Paul Swannell	Paul S.
Hilary Roberts	**Hilary R.**		
John Robinson	John R.	Soraya Tate	Soraya T.
Celia Robinson	Celia R.	Sarah Taylor	Sarah T.
Alan Robinson	Alan R.	JulieThompson	Julie T.
Matty Rogers	Matty R.	Keith Tilley	Keith T
Linda Rowlinson	Linda R.	Sue Timms	Sue T.
Richard Russell	Richard R.	Jennifer Todd	Jennifer T.
		Graham T.	Graham T.
Gloria Sanderson	Gloria S.	Liz Toomey	Liz T.
Donna Scott	Donna S.	Ian Turner	Ian T.
June Scott	June S.	Colin Twisleton	Colin T.
Hilary Scrivens	Hilary S.	Steve Twisleton	Steve Tw.
Darren Seaber	Darren S.		
John Shaw	John Sw.	Mandy Udhus	Many U.
Mark Simm	Mark S.		
Georgina Sherwood		Shirley Vickers	Shirley V.
	Georgina S.		
Sharon Sherwood	Sharon S.	Lesley Waite	Lesley W.
Martin Skinner	Martin S.	David Watcham	David Wm.
Kevin Slaymaker	Kevin S.	Stephen Watson	Stephen W.
Hazel Smith	Hazel S.	Sam Watts	Sam W.
Janet Smith	Janet S.	Steve Watts	Steve W.
Ian Smith	Ian S.	Karen Waugh	Karen W.
Graham Smith	Graham S.	David Weatherhead	
Andy Smith	Andy S.		David Wd.
Pamela Johnstone	Pamela J.	Phillip Webb	Phillip W.
Ian Smith	Ian S.	Maurice Webb	Maurice W.
Sheila Stanbridge	Sheila Se.	Heather Webberly	Heather W.
Terence Stanton	Terence S.	Dean West	Dean W.
Dorothy Stapleton		Derek Whiteside	Derek W.
	Dorothy S.	Ian Whiting	Ian W.
Jackie Steensel	Jackie S.	Peter Whiting	Peter W.
John Stephenson	John S.	Tracy Wilkins	Tracy W.
Tracy Stephenson	Tracey S.	Elvia Willems	Elvia W.
Derrick Stone	Derrick S.	Lorna Williams	Lorna W.

David Wilmin   David Wn.
Michael Wilson   Michael W.
Theresa Wilson   Theresa W.
Julie Woodruff   Julie W,
Geoffrey Woodward
                  Geoffrey W.
Mike Wright   Mike W.

Anthony Zastawny
                  Anthony Z.

Books on Wolverton

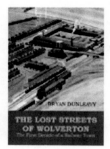

The Lost Streets of Wolverton
Bryan Dunleavy

This book tells the story of the creation of England's first company railway town, almost 175 years ago. It describes the decisions which led to its location, the ad hoc planning which led to this new community and its growth and development in its first decade. The works, the housing, the shops and most of the amenities have since disappeared as a consequence of new development and the book is a valuable reconstruction of the early town from preserved documents and reports.
ISBN 978-1-909054-004

Mainou's Manor
Bryan Dunleavy

The book describes the history of the manor of Wolverton from its earliest archaeological evidence through the centuries up to 1838, when it was completely transformed by the arrival of the railway.

ISBN 978-1-909054-059

First Impressions
Bryan Dunleavy

The book presents contemporary accounts of the new town of Wolverton upon its creation 175 years ago in 1838.

ISBN 978-1-909054-066

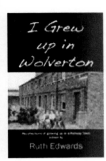

I Grew Up in Wolverton

Ruth Edwards

A compilation of Facebook conversations about growing up in Wolverton covering the second half of the 20th century.

ISBN 978-1-909054-035

Full details about books in print and forthcoming books from Magic Flute Publications may be found at www.magicflutepublications.co.uk

Lightning Source UK Ltd.
Milton Keynes UK
UKOW05f1517021213

222220UK00001B/3/P